Monuments and Memorials
of Philadelphia

4880 Lower Valley Road • Atglen, PA 19310

Allan M. Heller

MW01154916

Published by Schiffer Publishing, Ltd.
4880 Lower Valley Road
Atglen, PA 19310
Phone: (610) 593-1777;
Fax: (610) 593-2002
E-mail: Info@schifferbooks.com

For the largest selection of fine reference books on this and related subjects, please visit our website at www.schifferbooks.com. You may also write for a free catalog.

This book may be purchased from the publisher.
Please try your bookstore first.

We are always looking for people to write books on new and related subjects. If you have an idea for a book, please contact us at proposals@schifferbooks.com

Schiffer Books are available at special discounts for bulk purchases for sales promotions or premiums. Special editions, including personalized covers, corporate imprints, and excerpts can be created in large quantities for special needs. For more information contact the publisher.

In Europe, Schiffer books are distributed by
Bushwood Books
6 Marksbury Ave.
Kew Gardens
Surrey TW9 4JF England
Phone: 44 (0) 20 8392 8585; Fax: 44 (0) 20 8392 9876
E-mail: info@bushwoodbooks.co.uk
Website: www.bushwoodbooks.co.uk

Map data copyright OpenStreetMap contributors, CC-BY-SA.
openstreetmap.org creativecommons.org

Other Schiffer Books by the Author:
Monuments and Memorials of Washington, D.C. ISBN: 978-0-7643-3654-6. $19.99
Philadelphia Area Cemeteries. ISBN: 0-7643-2222-2. $12.95

Other Schiffer Books on Related Subjects:
Art in Savannah: A Guide to the Monuments, Museums, Galleries, and Other Places.
    Sandra L. Underwood. ISBN: 0-7643-2649-3. $14.95
Historic Architecture in Northwest Philadelphia: 1690 to 1930s. Joseph Minardi.
    ISBN: 978-0-7643-4198-4. $50.00
Historic Architecture in West Philadelphia, 1789-1930s. Joseph Minardi.
    ISBN: 978-0-7643-3771-0. $50.00
Philadelphia Haunts. Katharine Sarro. ISBN: 978-0-7643-2987-6. $14.99
Philadelphia Originals. Joseph Glantz. ISBN: 978-0-7643-3338-5. $34.99
Savannah Squares: A Keepsake Tour of Gardens, Architecture, and Monuments.
    Rob Hill. ISBN: 0-7643-2047-5. $9.95

Copyright © 2012 by Allan M. Heller

Library of Congress Control Number: 2012949351

All rights reserved. No part of this work may be reproduced or used in any form or by any means—graphic, electronic, or mechanical, including photocopying or information storage and retrieval systems—without written permission from the publisher.

The scanning, uploading and distribution of this book or any part thereof via the Internet or via any other means without the permission of the publisher is illegal and punishable by law. Please purchase only authorized editions and do not participate in or encourage the electronic piracy of copyrighted materials.

"Schiffer," "Schiffer Publishing, Ltd. & Design," and the "Design of pen and inkwell" are registered trademarks of Schiffer Publishing, Ltd.

Designed by RoS
Type set in Bernhard Modern BT/NewBskvll BT

ISBN: 978-0-7643-4223-3
Printed in China

Dedication

For Tati.

Acknowledgments

My gratitude goes out to the following individuals for their assistance and contributions:

Alex Bartlett, archivist/librarian, Germantown Historical Society; past and present members of Wordwrights writers' group in Exton, Pennsylvania; Judy Glass, Venturi, Scott Brown and Associates, Inc.; Peter J. Obst, Poles in America Foundation, Inc.; David Cruz, Director of Photography, Al Dia News; Anna Jensky; Roman Blazic; Teresa Siwak, editor of The Way newspaper; Jay Nachman, National Museum of American Jewish History; Michael Starr, Marketing Coordinator, JeffGraphics; Keisha Wiggins, Jefferson University; Debbie Feldman, Temple University Beasley School of Law; Lisa Carey, Boy Scouts of America; Cradle of Liberty Council; Patricia McBee, Executive Director, Friends Center; Vlad Ringe; Susannah Carroll and John Alviti, The Franklin Institute; Rabbi Albert Gabbai, Congregation Mikveh Israel; Ralph J. Rogers; Stan Horwitz; John Kahler, Director of Communications, Lutheran Theological Seminary; David G. Goldstein; Rev. David R. Adam, the Simpson House; Melissa A. Heinlein, Philadelphia VA Medical Center; Tatiana Heller; Elena "Mama" Greendlinger.

Contents

Introduction

My name is Ozymandias, King of Kings / Look on my Works, ye Mighty, and despair!

—*Shelley*

Monuments and memorials spring up throughout the country, the entire world, in areas urban and suburban. They range from the simplest structural adornments, such as the Clark Park Civil War Memorial—basically a rock on a pedestal—to the elaborate, eclectic Washington Monument in Eakins Oval, consisting of embossed plaques, three discrete fountains, over a dozen peripheral figures, and a majestic equestrian statue at the peak. Most take years from conception to execution: the basic structures due to bureaucratic hassles, and the more extravagant ones because of logistics and cost. But for all of the preliminary troubles that they may generate, monuments and memorials are usually improvements rather than impediments.

War is a popular inspiration for public sculptures, and of the 130 pieces profiled in this book, 42 deal with military subjects: conflicts minor and major, groups of soldiers within the armed forces, and especially generals and other officers. The latter overlaps with another subject typically memorialized in stone or bronze: famous individuals. Philadelphia has its share of eminent citizens recognized for their battlefield tactics, business acumen, philanthropy or political *savoir faire*. Historic events are frequently commemorated, sometimes without taking into consideration all of the facts surrounding these happenings. Even when tragedies are chronicled in immutable materials, they are presented with an underlying sense of hope, healing, and resilience. Cases in point are the Irish Memorial on Penn's Landing, and the Monument to the Six Million Jewish Martyrs on the Benjamin Franklin Parkway.

What qualifies as a monument or memorial? The Liberty Bell is featured in this book because it is such an enduring symbol of both Philadelphia and this great country (although the bell predates the establishment of the United States, and originally had nothing to do with liberty). Rocky Balboa, near the Art Museum, may seem undeserving of the distinction of monument, but is inextricably associated with the City of Brotherly Love. Even Claes Oldenburg's enormous steel clothespin at 15th and Market streets is accorded monument status in this humble offering. So too is Robert Indiana's famous *Love* sculpture. However, there are many public sculptures and works of art which, impressive though they may be, do not qualify as monuments or memorials *per se*.

The forms various monuments and memorials take, as well as the materials from which they are fashioned, have changed over the years. Bronze as a medium has long supplanted granite or marble, although the latter two are often incorporated for pedestals or bases. Classical motifs and pairing subjects with allegorical representations of traits or ideals were popular in the nineteenth century. Abstract depictions had little if any presence: the conventional approach was that a monument or memorial should look like its subject, or at least easily convey to the viewer who (or what) that subject was. The current and previous century have given us many abstract pieces that can transcend the limitations of traditional artistic renderings. Admittedly, the subjects of these pieces usually cannot be identified without the accompanying plaque or inscription.

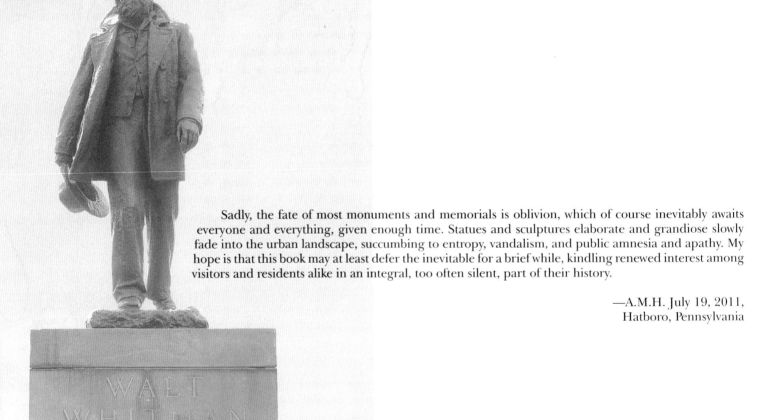

Sadly, the fate of most monuments and memorials is oblivion, which of course inevitably awaits everyone and everything, given enough time. Statues and sculptures elaborate and grandiose slowly fade into the urban landscape, succumbing to entropy, vandalism, and public amnesia and apathy. My hope is that this book may at least defer the inevitable for a brief while, kindling renewed interest among visitors and residents alike in an integral, too often silent, part of their history.

—A.M.H. July 19, 2011,
Hatboro, Pennsylvania

Art Museum 1

Captain John Ericsson Fountain

"Dedicated to the memory of Captain John Ericsson, scientist, inventor, patriot. Born in Sweden July 31, 1803. Died in America, the country of his adoption, March 8, 1889." *Photo courtesy of Tatiana Heller.*

With the only discernible difference being the inscription around the berm of the main basin, the fountain commemorating Swedish engineer John Ericsson (1803-1889) might be termed a sister fountain to that of Eli Kirk Price, Jr. The fountains are situated on either side of the Washington Monument, and were both completed the same year (1934) by the same architectural trio, consisting of Horace Trumbauer, Alfred Zantziger, and Charles E. Borie, Jr. "Dedicated to the memory of Captain John Ericsson, scientist, inventor, patriot. Born in Sweden July 31, 1803. Died in America, the country of his adoption, March 8, 1889."

Ericsson, who had been a captain in the Swedish army, emigrated to the United States in 1839. He is best known for his improvement of the screw propeller, a crucial advancement in an era of naval warfare development. He is often mistaken as the inventor of this propulsion device. In 1861, Ericsson assisted the United States Navy with his design of the iron-clad Monitor, largely in response to the Confederate's Merrimac. The two ships fought a famous battle in March 1862.

An ornate, $60,000 granite monument to the esteemed Swedish engineer by James Earle Fraser was dedicated in 1926 in Washington, D.C.

Location: West end of Eakins Oval, Benjamin Franklin Parkway and 24th Street.

Charioteer of Delphi

The inscription reads: "From the cradle of democracy in the ancient world to the cradle of democracy in the new world. From the people of Greece to the people of America."

Presented in 1976 to the city of Philadelphia by the Greek people, this bronze statue is a reproduction of the ancient Greek original, which was made circa the fifth century B.C., and most likely depicted the charioteer holding in his outstretched right hand the reins of a team of four horses, who were of course drawing a chariot. Beside the charioteer would have been a groom for the horses. The original Charioteer of Delphi was unearthed in the late nineteenth century by a team of French archaeologists (FPAA), and is on display at the Delphi Archaeological Museum. The piece was commissioned to commemorate a chariot race victory in the Pythian Games, which were held every four years in honor of the god Apollo. Part of an inscription recovered references Polyzalos—known as "the Tyrant of Gela"—a Sicilian dictator who ruled the city of Gela for about twelve years. The Charioteer stands five feet, nine inches, atop an approximately two foot black marble pedestal. The long, short-sleeved, pleated gown that he is wearing is known as a xystis, and was typical garb for charioteers (Opper).

The Philadelphia facsimile was made by Greek sculptors Theodora Papayannis and Nikos Kerlis via the lost wax process (Bach: 245).

Location: East side of the Art Museum, 24th Street and Benjamin Franklin Parkway.

The Charioteer of Delphi—actually a very convincing facsimile of an ancient original.

Eli Kirk Price, Jr. Fountain

The inner basin of the *Eli Kirk Price, Jr. Fountain*. The equestrian statue of Philadelphia's Washington Monument is visible in the background. *Photo courtesy of Tatiana Heller.*

Tourists are more likely than city residents to stroll the perimeter of this memorial fountain to one of Philadelphia's great civic leaders, reading the gold-lettered inscription paraphrasing the man's accomplishments in a mere twenty-four words: "In memory of Eli Kirk Price (1860–1933) whose wisdom and dedication were responsible for the development of the Parkway and the Art Museum."

Eli Kirk Price, Jr. was the grandson of a prominent attorney who founded Fairmount Park. Like his grandfather, Price practiced law and maintained an active role in the development of his city. As vice president of the Fairmount Park Commission, Price was responsible for securing funding for the construction of the Philadelphia Museum of Art, as well as for the Benjamin Franklin Bridge. In 1928, he received the Philadelphia Award for his good citizenship. Other recipients of this award—started in 1921 by author and publisher Edward W. Bok—have included singer Marian Anderson, conductor Eugene Ormandy, developer Willard Rouse, and Mayor (and future governor of Pennsylvania) Edward G. Rendell.

Price's son, Philip, was also an attorney, and served as president of the Fairmount Park Commission from 1954 to 1969. Philip died in 1989 at the age of 91.

The *Eli Kirk Price, Jr. Fountain* was completed in 1934, and like the Captain John Ericsson Fountain, was a collaboration between architects Horace Trumbauer, Alfred Zantziger, and Charles E. Borie, Jr. The Ericsson and Price Fountains flank the Washington Monument.

Location: West end of Eakins Oval, Benjamin Franklin Parkway, and 24th Street.

Ernesta Drinker Ballard Memorial

A modest urn pays tribute to the woman who served for over twenty years as a Fairmount Park commissioner, and was one of the founders of the Fairmount Park Conservancy. In the former capacity, Ballard spearheaded the restoration of several Philadelphia landmarks, among them the Swann Memorial Fountain in Logan Square. Local organizations that she founded or cofounded include the Fairmount Park Historic Preservation Trust, and an urban beautification program called Philadelphia Green. During Ballard's seventeen years at the helm of the Pennsylvania Horticultural Society, the organization enjoyed significant growth. Prior to that, Ballard operated a horticultural business for ten years.

Ballard's activities extended far beyond plants and flowers. An ardent feminist, she was heavily involved with the National Organization for Women (NOW) and the National Abortion Rights Action League (NARAL), where she was chairwoman from 1989 to 1991.

Ballard's drive and dedication garnered her numerous accolades. In 1976 she received a Gimbel Award, given to accomplished Philadelphia women, and in 2001 she received the Philadelphia Award. Her aunt, author Catherine Drinker Bowen, also received a Gimbel Award. Ballard died in 2005 at the age of 85.

Location: Garden of Fairmount Water Works Interpretive Center, 640 Waterworks Drive, north of Art Museum Drive and west of Kelly Drive.

A modest urn pays tribute to the woman who served for over twenty years as a Fairmount Park commissioner, and was one of the founders of the Fairmount Park Conservancy. *Photo courtesy of Tatiana Heller.*

General Anthony Wayne

General Anthony Wayne, perched high upon his pedestal.

English sculptor John Gregory's bronze equestrian of the famous Revolutionary War general was installed in 1937, and regilded in 1968. Upon a thirteen-and-a-half foot granite pedestal, horse and rider seem remote and inaccessible. This memorial was part of a bequest from General William M. Reilly, calling for the erection of statues honoring several other Revolutionary War heroes as well, including Lafayette, Richard Montgomery, Casimir Pulaski, Friedrich von Steuben, Nathanael Greene, and John Paul Jones. Reilly died March 3, 1896, and was interred in Philadelphia's Laurel Hill Cemetery.

Born in Chester County, Pennsylvania, in 1745, Anthony Wayne proved to be the consummate soldier, who, although he had his defeats, demonstrated courage, competence, and leadership. The Paoli Massacre, which occurred the evening of September 20, 1777, was his only real fiasco, a bloody bayonet ambush by a large force of the British. The Americans suffered over 300 casualties; British losses were inconsequential. Incensed that some questioned his strategic capabilities in the wake of the disaster, Wayne himself insisted on being court-martialed, and was subsequently acquitted. "Mad Anthony" later redeemed himself with a similar attack on English troops on July 13, 1779, when he led 1300 men to capture Stony Point on the Hudson River. The British had recently taken this fort, along with West Point, six weeks earlier. After the war, Wayne resigned from the military.

After a few years in politics—in the Pennsylvania Assembly and in a truncated term in the Georgia Congress—Wayne tried his hand at farming and nearly went bankrupt. He returned to the only life that he really knew: soldiering. From 1792 to 1795, American troops under his command quelled a series of Native American uprisings in western Pennsylvania and Ohio. Wayne died on December 15, 1796.

Location: East terrace of Art Museum, 26th Street and Benjamin Franklin Parkway.

General Casimir Pulaski

A skilled horseman who was placed in charge of the American cavalry in 1777, Casimir Pulaski (1747–1779) might have been more appropriately represented by an equestrian statue. Instead he stands in a swaggering pose atop a seven-and-a-half-foot granite pedestal. His left hand rests on his hip, his right hand grips a long, curved blade two-thirds the length of his body. An inscription on the front of the pedestal supplies brief biographical information. The Pulaski statue was installed in 1947.

This Polish patriot had much in common with his countryman and fellow general Tadeusz Kosciusko (1746–1817), who also fought for his homeland's freedom in vain, and also came to the aid of the struggling Colonial forces. In Pulaski's case, he attempted to repulse the Russian invaders of Poland prior to his voyage to America, while Kosciuszko returned home after the American Revolution to aid the Poles in an ill-fated rebellion years later. Pulaski commanded the cavalry bravely at the battles of Brandywine and Germantown, although both engagements were defeats for the Continental Army. He was mortally wounded on October 9, 1779, in a joint attempt by American and French troops to retake the captured city of Savannah, Georgia, from the British.

The nine foot plus heroic bronze of Pulaski was designed by Amherst, Massachusetts, artist Sidney B. Waugh. Waugh, who studied abroad in Rome and Paris, spent the major part of his career employed as a designer at the Steuben Division of Corning Glass in New York. His portfolio included architectural commissions as well, such as sculptural enhancements for the National Archives, Post Office, and Federal Reserve buildings in the nation's capital (Monuments Men). He was elected a fellow of the National Sculpture Society in 1930.

Location: West side of Art Museum, Kelly Drive and 26th Street.

A proud Pulaski. *Photo courtesy of Peter J. Obst.*

General Friedrich von Steuben

Friedrich Wilhelm Ludolf Gerhard Augustin von Steuben (1730–1794) arrived in America in 1778, after meeting Benjamin Franklin in Paris a year prior. Franklin arranged for von Steuben's introduction to Washington, who appointed von Steuben Inspector General of American forces. In the army of Frederick the Great, von Steuben had only been a captain, but he had seen action during the Seven Years War (known in the Colonies as The French and Indian Wars), and fought in Europe between a coalition of Prussia and Britain versus Russia, Austria, and France). Although Franklin significantly exaggerated the credentials of the stoic Prussian officer, von Steuben did manage to instill in Washington's army much-needed discipline and military demeanor. Since von Steuben spoke German and French, he instructed—and occasionally swore at—the troops at Valley Forge through a translator. For his services to the cause of American Independence, von Steuben was granted a $2,500 annual pension, a 16,000-acre estate in New York, and United States citizenship. Von Steuben's accumulated regulations for drilling and military protocol comprised his 1794 manual *Regulations for the Order and Discipline of the Troops of the United States*, which remained the army's official guide until 1812.

Warren Wheelock's nine-and-a-half-foot bronze sculpture of the Prussian general, part of the William M. Reilly Memorial, was installed in 1947. The granite pedestal, like those for the statues of Montgomery, Pulaski, and Lafayette, were designed by architect C. Louis Borie (Bach: 228).

Location: Art Museum, Kelly Drive and 26th Street.

For his services to the cause of American Independence, von Steuben was granted a $2,500 annual pension, a 16,000-acre estate in New York, and United States citizenship. *Photo courtesy of Peter J. Obst.*

General Nathanael Greene

A long, lanky Nathanael Greene stands with his hands behind his back, and one foot forward—a contemplative rather than a decisive pose. He appears taller than his fellow generals of the William M. Reilly Memorial—Pulaski, von Steuben, Lafayette, and Jones—but at nine foot three inches is actually the shortest of the bronze statues in this collection. Greene's memorial was completed in 1960. The granite pedestal bears inscriptions on the front and sides, the former his most famous quote: "We fight, get beat, rise, and fight again." Savannah, Georgia, and Washington, D.C. also have memorials to Greene.

Greene (1742–1786), a former Quaker, was Quartermaster General of the troops at Valley Forge during the brutal winter of 1777 to 1778. At the onset of the American Revolution, Greene had been instrumental in starting the Rhode Island Militia. By 1780, he was leading American forces in the south in a series of hit-and-run clashes against British general Charles Cornwallis. Although Greene preferred to winnow down the enemy, he and his men were forced into a major confrontation with Cornwallis on March 15, 1781, a confrontation that resulted in an American loss, but a British Pyrrhic victory. Greene was a close friend of Washington, and such was his admiration for his commander that he named his son George Washington Greene.

Sculptor Lewis Iselin, Jr., a World War II naval veteran, is also known for designing a nine foot marble statue representing Memory and two reliefs for an American military cemetery in Suresnes, France, near Paris. He was awarded the contract by the American Battle Monuments Commission. In a 1969 interview, Iselin explained that the works were for part of a building that commemorated soldiers whose bodies were not recovered. "[S]o many people were just blown to bits that something had to be done about the people whose bodies were lost" (Smithsonian). Iselin was awarded a Guggenheim Fellowship in 1952. He died in Camden, Maine, in 1990, at the age of 77.

■ **Location:** Art museum, Kelly Drive and 26th Street.

General Nathanael Greene by Lewis Iselin, Jr.

General Richard Montgomery

This memorial, erected circa 1946, is by J. Wallace Kelly, who also created the figure of the *Ploughman* for the Ellen Phillips Samuel Memorial. Kelly was born in Secane, Pennsylvania, but grew up in Philadelphia. In 1916, while a student at the Pennsylvania Academy of Fine Arts, he was awarded a Cresson Scholarship. This consisted of a $600 stipend, equivalent to about $12,000 today, adjusted for inflation (Bureau of Labor Statistics).

The promising military career of charismatic Irish-born General Richard Montgomery (1738–1775) was cut short on December 31, 1775, during the failed siege of Quebec by American forces. The plan, hatched in September of that year, was an unprecedented one, but one that could have potentially crippled the enemy early in the conflict. The Americans were emboldened by their successes at Fort Ticonderoga and Crown Point, and these were to be launching points for Montgomery's troops, who would be conveyed via the major waterways to Canada's interior. Montgomery's men took forts Chamblee and St. John, as well as the city of Montreal, before advancing toward their main objective.

Benedict Arnold, then a colonel, had earlier led a force from Gardiners Town (today's Gardiner), Maine, and planned to rendezvous with Montgomery in Canada. After weeks of enduring frigid weather and starvation on the long march, fewer than half of Arnold's troops reached the outskirts of Quebec. Lacking supplies as well as men, they were forced to wait for Montgomery. The two contingents of American troops began an assault on Quebec on New Year's Eve, 1775. Montgomery and his second-in-command were instantly struck down by grapeshot from a British cannon, at which point the rest of his forces retreated. Unaware that Montgomery had fallen, Arnold pressed on, until he was shot in the leg and carried off the field by his men. The siege of Quebec was a disastrous defeat for the Colonial forces. As for Arnold, he would live to distinguish himself at the Battle of Saratoga in 1777, and to disgrace himself with the attempted turnover of West Point to the British in 1780.

Location: Art museum, Kelly Drive and 26th Street.

Even the martyred Montgomery's statue looks forlorn.

Joan of Arc

Perhaps Samuel G. Thompson, in accepting this monument on behalf of the Fairmount Park Art Association, misspoke when he implied that the addition of Joan of Arc was an improvement to city statuary, by stating, "We already have enough statues personifying destruction, such as beasts of prey, savages, and men of war" (NewsBank). Not that Parisian sculptor Emmanuel Fremiet's bronze equestrian was unimpressive, or that the feats of his subject, a simple peasant girl from Domremy, were not miraculous. But although more venerated than most "men of war," Joan—depicted in full battle regalia astride a similarly-caparisoned steed—is as much a martial figure as she is a divine one. Her mailed left hand clutches the reins, while her bare right hand holds aloft a mighty lance. At her side, a sword in a scabbard waits to be drawn. Her suit of armor practically obscures all traces of femininity, with the possible exception of the inconspicuous ponytail draped down her back. Her face is smooth, firm, and intrepid.

Believing that she was on a mission from God and guided by the saints, the young French maiden rallied her country from the brink of defeat during the Hundred Years War with England. Captured by the Burgundians—who were allied with the English—she was convicted of witchcraft and condemned to death. Joan was promised clemency if she confessed and subsequently renounced her "crimes," but she refused. She was burned at the stake at Rouen in 1431. In 1920, she was canonized.

The unveiling of Fremiet's *Joan of Arc* was held on November 15, 1890. About 3,000 people attended, listening to speeches in both English and French. In 1872, Fremiet had received a commission for an equestrian Joan of Arc, to be placed in the Place des Pyramides in Paris. The completed monument was installed in February of 1874. Although Fremiet based his Philadelphia statue on the original, there were minor differences. The Fairmount Park Art Association initially sought to purchase the Place des Pyramides Joan of Arc. In 1899, the sculptor had the original melted down, and recast with the specifications used for the one in Philadelphia. In July of 2009, the Philadelphia Joan of Arc was temporarily removed for renovations, and returned to her place the following April.

Location: 25th Street and Kelly Drive.

Behold the patron saint of France, in all her gilded glory.

John Marshall

Installed in 1931, this statue of John Marshall is a replica of one placed at the Capitol in Washington, D.C. in 1884. The inscription reads, "Chief Justice of the United States 1801-1835. As a soldier he fought that the nation might come into being. As expounder of the Constitution he gave it length of days." Marshall is depicted seated, in his judicial robes.

The sculptor for the original memorial was William Wetmore Story. Born in Salem, Massachusetts, Story was the grandson and son of a judge. His father, Joseph Story, was an associate justice who served with Marshall, and is the youngest person ever to have been appointed to the Supreme Court. William Wetmore Story's son, T. Waldo Story, also became a sculptor.

Born in Virginia in 1755, John Marshall went on to serve his burgeoning nation as a soldier, statesman, and finally, judge. He became a lawyer following his stint in the Continental Army, setting up his own practice in his home state. Marshall deeply admired George Washington, and shortly after his tenure as chief justice began, wrote a multi-volume biography of the late commander-in-chief. Marshall was the fourth chief justice of the Supreme Court, and still holds the record as the longest-serving chief justice, and the second longest-serving of all Supreme Court justices, behind William O. Douglas (1939–1975). Prior to his term on the nation's highest court, Marshall's political career included membership in the Virginia Assembly, the U.S. House of Representatives, and briefly, as the Secretary of State under President John Adams. He died in Philadelphia at the age of 79, following a stagecoach accident.

Location: Behind the Philadelphia Museum of Art, 26th Street and Benjamin Franklin Parkway.

This statue of John Marshall is a replica of one placed at the Capitol in Washington, D.C., in 1884.

John Paul Jones

The inscription at the base of the *John Paul Jones* statue recalls the commodore's greatest wartime triumph, that over the British ship *Serapis* in September of 1779. Only the stout Scotsman's determination enabled him to predict that he would miraculously be able to snatch victory from the jaws of defeat. Not only did he refuse British captain Richard Pearson's suggestion that he "strike his colors," but Jones forced Pearson and his crew to surrender instead. Jones supposedly replied, "I have not yet begun to fight!" At the time of the battle, Jones was a captain in the Continental Navy, and in command of the ship *Bonhomme Richard*.

Completed in 1957 by Walker Hancock (see Pennsylvania Railroad War Memorial), this heroic bronze depicts Jones in naval uniform, a sheathed sword at his left flank, and either about to look through his spyglass at the enemy ship, or having just done so.

Born in Scotland on July 6, 1747, John Paul (who later tacked on "Jones" to his name) emigrated to America as a young man. Already an experienced sailor when he arrived (it was not unusual for boys as young as twelve or thirteen to go to sea), Jones progressed steadily in the ranks of the fledgling American navy. After the Revolution, Jones joined the Russian navy. He died in 1792 at the age of forty-five. In 1905, his remains were exhumed from a graveyard in France, and reburied on the grounds of the United States Naval Academy in Annapolis, Maryland.

Location: South of Kelly Drive and west of 26th Street.

"I have not yet begun to fight!" John Paul Jones, September, 1779.
Photo courtesy of Peter J. Obst.

Lafayette

Although Gilbert de Lafayette (1757–1834) has been described as flamboyant, Raoul Josset's statute of the French general—completed in 1943 and installed in 1947—goes a bit too far. His head—disproportionately small in comparison with his body—is slightly cocked to the left, a foppish smirk on his bemused face. His right arm is flung in mid-air at a 45-degree angle, and except for the position of his feet, he seems about to execute a ballerina's twirl. The marquis also appears to be in the process of shedding his cloak, a feat which the position of his left hand and sword would preclude. From the back, the folds of Lafayette's cloak give him an avian appearance (Buten).

Josset won a national competition to design the *Lafayette* statue. At just under 10-1/2 feet, it is the largest of those included in the *William M. Reilly Memorial*, but small in scope when compared to the more than twenty public monuments that Josset designed prior to *Lafayette's*, both in the United States and his native France. Josset emigrated to the United States and became a citizen, settling eventually in Texas. There he received several commissions for monuments with themes related to the state's political and military history, among them a huge pink granite grave marker for the victims of an 1836 massacre of 342 Texan prisoners by the forces of General Antonio Lopez de Santa Anna. (The defenders who perished at the Alamo that same year numbered around 180 by most accounts.)

In February of 1778, France officially allied itself with the Americans in the latter's war of independence, but the noble Lafayette arrived in America in 1777, whereupon he was appointed a major general in the Continental army. He fought in the Battle of Brandywine on September 11, and took a musket ball in the leg. In a letter to his wife, the twenty-year-old general dismissed the injury as a mere flesh wound. Unlike other foreign military figures, who sought recompense for their assistance, Lafayette volunteered his services to the struggling Colonies. While several prominent Frenchmen, such as Rochambeau and Comte de Grasse, aided the American cause, none are as remembered or revered as Lafayette.

Location: South of Kelly Drive and west of 26th Street.

Major General Peter Muhlenberg

Born John Peter Gabriel Muhlenberg on October 1, 1746, in Trappe, Montgomery County, Pennsylvania, Muhlenberg was the son of Henry Melchior Muhlenberg, the founder of the Lutheran Church in America, and Anna Weiser. At the time of his death in 1807, Peter Muhlenberg was president of the Incorporated German Society in Philadelphia, the organization that sponsored his memorial. This statue, by J. Otto Schweizer, was unveiled at City Hall's south plaza on October 6, 1910, and in the 1960s was placed in storage during construction of the Municipal Services Building.

A famous anecdote concerning the preacher turned soldier relates how at the conclusion of a sermon in his church at Woodstock, Virginia, in 1776, Reverend Muhlenberg paraphrased Ecclesiastes 3:8, telling the congregation: "There is a time to preach and a time to fight. Now is the time to fight." With that, he cast off his black minister's gown to reveal the uniform of a Continental Army officer. Departing with a flourish, he entreated his parishioners to join him in his country's struggle. The gown that Muhlenberg wore for the last time that day appeared 134 years later, during an unveiling of a monument to the patriot preacher. Common Pleas Court Judge William H. Staake, addressing the crowd of 30,000 who turned out for the dedication, held the famous garment aloft after recounting the legendary tale. Schweizer's statue depicts Muhlenberg at that historic moment. Panels on the front and side present Muhlenberg's life as a preacher, soldier and statesman.

Among those in attendance that October 6—"German Day"—included Schweizer, the German consul Arthur Murda, representatives from German and American veterans' organizations, a parade division from the Ancient Order of Hibernians, members of the Muhlenberg Monument Committee, two of Muhlenberg's great-great grandsons, a great-great-great granddaughter, and Mayor John E. Reyburn, who accepted the statue for his city.

Today the Muhlenberg memorial stands behind the Philadelphia Museum of Art, all but forgotten.

Location: Behind the Art Museum, 25th Street and Kelly Drive.

Preacher and patriot Peter Muhlenberg.

Young Meher
(Armenian Genocide Monument)

Young Meher commemorates the Armenian holocaust.

Installed in 1976, this monument commemorates both the American bicentennial and the 61st anniversary of the Armenian genocide, which occurred during World War I and has been called the first Holocaust of the twentieth century. Over one million Armenians were killed by the Turkish regime. The inscription lists April 24, 1915, as the beginning of the genocide, the so-called "Day of Infamy." The central figure for the memorial is a twenty-two foot bronze statue of Meher—a legendary Armenian hero. Themed plaques on all four sides of the pedestal depict spiritual and historical scenes pertaining to the Armenian people.

For hundreds of years, the Armenians were under the rule of the vast Ottoman Empire, and as Christians, they and other non-Muslims were second-class citizens. When finally, near the end of the nineteenth century Armenians began to clamor for equality, they were brutally suppressed. But more brutality lay in store with the rise of the Young Turk government about a decade later. Anti-Christian sentiment erupted in the wake of a disastrous war in 1912, in which the Ottoman Empire lost a huge amount of its territory to rebellion (OPB). Mass deportations and exiles of Armenians soon followed, as thousands of men, women, and children were forced from their homes and sent on death marches across the desert. Those who did not perish from exhaustion or starvation were often attacked by roving bands of criminals, while the Turkish gendarmes escorting the Armenian convoys turned a blind eye. To this day, the Turkish government officially denies the Armenian genocide.

The sculptor for this memorial was Khoren Der Harootian, an Armenian genocide survivor who lost over twenty members of his family. Der Harootian died in New York in 1991 following a car accident (derharootian.com).

Location: Art Museum and Kelly drives and 25th Street.

Rocky Balboa

Derided as a mere movie prop, and lauded as a Philadelphia icon, the 8-1/2-foot, 1,500-pound statue of Rocky Balboa stands triumphantly near the front steps of the Philadelphia Museum of Art, a short distance from where he originally was nearly thirty years ago. Actor Sylvester Stallone, who played the titular pugilist in no fewer than six films, commissioned Colorado sculptor A. Thomas Schomberg to create the piece for the 1982 premiere of the film Rocky III. Schomberg, who specializes in sports-themed artwork, created a total of three such statues, one of which is in the San Diego Hall of Champions Museum in California (Schomberg).

When Stallone tried to donate the statue to the Art Museum, he was at first rebuffed. Critics found the piece kitschy, overblown, and out of place. For a time Rocky was relocated to the Spectrum at Broad Street and Pattison Avenue. But by 2006, this legendary fictional Philadelphian had come nearly full circle, settling on a small plot of ground a short distance from his original digs. A typical day finds visitors lining up to pose for a photograph with the famous fighter, making it difficult to procure a picture of the bronze boxer sans admirers.

In the original movie, for which Stallone wrote the screenplay, Rocky Balboa is a two-bit boxer from South Philadelphia who works menial jobs to support himself. He has the potential, but lacks the drive to be a great fighter. Driven hard by his trainer, Mickey Goldmill (Burgess Meredith), and inspired by his girlfriend, Adrian Pennino (Talia Shire), Rocky finally gets a shot at fame when he is matched with World Heavyweight Champ Apollo Creed (Carl Weathers).

Location: East side of the Art Museum, 24th Street and Benjamin Franklin Parkway.

Does the *Rocky* statue really qualify as a monument or memorial? Sure!

Stephen Girard

Dedicated May 20, 1897, John Massey Rhind's heroic bronze of commerce magnate and philanthropist Stephen Girard (1750–1831) was the first of three memorials to the French-born Philadelphian. The statue had been hoisted into place atop its granite pedestal two days earlier, to await the unveiling at City Hall's west plaza. The day of the dedication was especially sultry for mid-spring, and the *Philadelphia Inquirer* reported that several people fainted from the heat and the stifling crowd. The date marked both the 147th anniversary of Girard's birth and the 50th anniversary of the official opening of Girard College (which was actually January 1, 1848).

A grand parade, consisting of marchers who were past and present students of Girard College, proceeded from City Hall to the Union League, where they were reviewed by Pennsylvania governor Daniel H. Hastings. Afterwards they returned to their point of departure to witness the unveiling ceremonies, during which Mayor Charles F. Warwick accepted the Girard statue on behalf of the city. Also present was former mayor Edwin S. Stuart, who served on the board of trustees that administered the fund for Girard College, sculptor Rhind, and the subject's grandniece, Ellen E. Girard. The statue was draped in the flags of France and the United States, representing both Girard's native and adopted countries.

Rhind's Girard has a patriarchal demeanor—that of an older, accomplished individual. His coat is open to reveal a vest, buttoned to the top. His right leg is slightly bent, adding a bit of energy to an otherwise static pose. Bronze panels on the sides of the pedestal illustrate scenes from Girard's life.

Rhind's later commissions in Philadelphia included memorials to Henry Howard Houston (1900), Tedyuscung (1902), and John Wanamaker (1923).

Location: Behind the Art Museum, 25th Street and Kelly Drive.

Stephen Girard (1750–1831), consummate capitalist, Philadelphia philanthropist.

Bronze panels on the sides of the pedestal depict scenes from the life of Stephen Girard.

Thomas Fitzsimmons

Sculpted by Giuseppe Donato, this monument was erected in 1946 by the Friendly Sons of Saint Patrick, an organization formed in Philadelphia in 1771 to help Irish immigrants, and of which Fitzsimmons was a member. A roughly eight foot bronze, Fitzsimmons is depicted with a quill in his right hand. The inscription on the front of the granite pedestal reads:

THOMAS FITZSIMMONS / BORN IN IRELAND 1741 / DIED IN PHILADELPHIA 1811 / MEMBER OF THE CONTINENTAL CONGRESS / SIGNER OF THE CONSTITUTION / OF THE UNITED STATES / MEMBER OF THE 1ST, 2ND, AND 3RD CONGRESS.

His adopted country was good to Fitzsimmons, who soon prospered as a merchant after his arrival in Philadelphia in 1760, and he gave back to both his nation and his community a hundredfold. During the war with England, Fitzsimmons contributed his time and money to the cause of American independence; he even formed and commanded a local militia. As a politician, the feisty Fitzsimmons held strong opinions which he was not shy about voicing, particularly during the 1787 Constitutional Convention. An outspoken Federalist, he allied himself with Alexander Hamilton in advocating a strong central government above individual states' rights. His political career spanned some twenty-five years, concluding in 1795 with the end of his term in the House of Representatives. In 1781, Fitzsimmons helped charter a national bank, for which Robert Morris drafted the plans. Fitzsimmons was also a devout Catholic, a noted philanthropist, and a proponent of public education. He died in Philadelphia on August 26, 1811.

Location: East side of Logan Square, west of 18th Street, between Race and Vine streets.

This monument was erected by the Friendly Sons of Saint Patrick. *Photo courtesy of Tatiana Heller.*

Washington Monument

The nation's capital is not the only city to boast a memorial to the foremost founding father; Philadelphia's Washington Monument was dedicated on May 15, 1897, eighty-seven years after the sponsoring organization officially announced their intentions. The creation of German sculptor Rudolf Siemering, the work is an intricate, artistic masterpiece which sadly, with the passing of over a century, is taken for granted by locals and even visitors to the city. The central, equestrian figure viewers will probably recognize as General George Washington, and while they may marvel at the complexity of the monument, they will fail to grasp the historical and symbolic significance of the surrounding sculptures. But such is the fate of many, perhaps most, public monuments.

Siemering's enthusiasm for the project is evident, even decades later. The base is comprised of thirteen granite steps, representing the original colonies, which lead up to recumbent bronze animals on the corners of the monument. On the next level, water flows from fountains on all sides, paired with sculptures of Native Americans and frontiersmen. Atop a thirty foot pedestal sits a seventeen foot Washington astride his horse.

Close-up photographs reveal the painstaking detail on Washington's face, as well as that of his mount, but this is unfortunately out of most visitors' range of vision. The pedestal is adorned with bas-reliefs on either side, and allegorical representations on the front and back. A portion of the monument—the bronze group on the back of the pedestal known as "America Awakening Her Sons to Fight for Liberty"—was exhibited in 1891 in Siemering's native Berlin (Newsbank).

For his *Washington Monument*, Siemering was heavily influenced by an equestrian statue in Berlin of Frederick the Great by Christian Rauch, with whom Siemering's mentor, Gustav Blaser, had studied (Wainwright: 134).

A pair of bronze stags near the base of Philadelphia's *Washington Monument*.

Erected by the Pennsylvania Society of the Cincinnati, Philadelphia's *Washington Monument* was originally located at the Green Street entrance to Fairmount Park.

Location: West end of Eakins Oval, Benjamin Franklin Parkway and 24th Street.

A bronze panel detail.

Philadelphia's *Washington Monument* is much more interesting than a huge marble obelisk.

Aero Memorial

The *Aero Memorial*. Globe by Paul Manship, plinth by Joseph P. Sims. *Photo courtesy of Peter J. Obst.*

From the center of a plaza on 20th Street and Benjamin Franklin Parkway, across from the Franklin Institute, sprouts a black granite column capped by a filigreed golden globe, within whose confines are myriad Zodiac figures—fish, birds, snakes, and dragons. Pinned unobtrusively between the base of the globe and the top of the shaft is a woman reclining on her side, her eyes covered with a shroud, her torso bare. Embossed in bright golden letters on the front of the column is "*Aero Memorial / World War I / 1917–1918.*" On the back of the column are the names of six fallen American flyers: Julian Biddle, Richard Foulke Day, Norton Downs, Jr., Carl Christian Glanz, William Besse Kuen, and Houston Woodward. The surrounding stone walls bear inscriptions from Shakespeare, among other writers. This spot is known as Aviator Park.

In 1917, the Aero Club of Pennsylvania indirectly initiated plans for this tribute to aviators killed in action during World War I. As of the following January, the *Aero Memorial* Fund contained a mere $100. By the time the memorial was dedicated on June 1, 1950, another world war had been fought, and the total cost of the *Aero Memorial* came to $35,000. This was shared by the Fairmount Park Association and the Aero Club (Aero Club of Pennsylvania). The six foot diameter globe was regilded in 2000. The black granite plinth was designed by Joseph P. Sims.

Sculptor Paul Manship intended the globe to symbolize the Celestial Sphere, and he painstakingly researched all aspects of the Zodiac in order to produce what he considered a flawless representation. According to historian Rebecca Reynolds, "They chose a celestial sphere presumably because it's where aviators are; they're in the sky [...] In fact, to have the night sky represent fallen aviators is rather poetic." Eagle-eyed observers—or those who know exactly where to look—may notice at the base of the sphere a figure of a bearded man, with hair just touching his shoulders. Manship intended this figure to be a representation of himself (FPAA).

Location: 20th Street between Race Street and Benjamin Franklin Parkway, across the street from the Franklin Institute.

All Wars Memorial to Colored Soldiers and Sailors

Blacks have served in every major conflict in which the United States was involved, from the earliest stirrings of the American Revolution to the present day. During the War of Independence a number of slaves obtained their freedom in return for military service (an offer also extended by the British). Blacks were permitted to join the Union cause about halfway through the Civil War, and their competence and courage refuted the claims of their detractors. Still, a long time would pass before Black servicemen would received the recognition that they deserved, and many Blacks took exception to an editorial by W.E.B. Du Bois in the July 1918 issue of *Crisis*, the official publication of the National Association for the Advancement of Colored People (NAACP), in which the author entreated Blacks to fully support the United States during the First World War, despite the nation's rampant racism (Summit: 63).

Situated around and atop a huge granite block are numerous bronze figures designed by sculptor J. Otto Schweizer, whose works in Philadelphia include the Henry Melchior Muhlenberg Memorial and that of Muhlenberg's son, Major General Peter Muhlenberg. Front and center is the personification of Justice, holding aloft two wreaths. Flanking her are groups of Black soldiers and sailors. Approximately twenty-two feet high, the *All Wars Memorial* is crowned with a flame surrounded by American eagles. In 1994 this piece was moved from Fairmount Park to its current site.

Aside from the obviously dated and offensive term "colored," part of an inscription on this memorial referencing the "World War" gives a clue as to the age of the structure, which was dedicated in 1934. Seven years earlier, the state of Pennsylvania appropriated $50,000 for the project, at the behest of a Black legislator and veteran.

Location: West side of Logan Square, southeast of 20th Street and Benjamin Franklin Parkway.

The *All Wars Memorial to Colored Soldiers and Sailors,* 1934, by J. Otto Schweizer.

James Earle Fraser's Benjamin Franklin sits regally in John T. Windrim's rotunda. *From the historical and interpretive collections of The Franklin Institute, Philadelphia, PA.*

Benjamin Franklin National Memorial

After having seen both the *Benjamin Franklin National Memorial* in Philadelphia and the *Lincoln Memorial* in Washington, D.C., one cannot help but draw certain parallels. Both are enshrined in structures inspired by ancient Greek models; architect John T. Windrim (the son of architect James H. Windrim) designed his magnificent marble rotunda that houses Franklin after the Pantheon, while Henry Bacon envisioned a colonnaded temple based on the Parthenon for Lincoln. The centerpiece of the Lincoln and the Franklin memorials consist of a roughly twenty foot seated marble likeness of each subject. But Daniel Chester French's massive marble Abe was completed in 1914, twenty-four years before James Earle Fraser's Franklin. And of course, Franklin and Lincoln were from two very different periods of American history, although both saw their country torn asunder by war and internal strife.

The seated statue of Franklin and its pedestal weigh a combined 120 tons, and were carved from white marble. The *Benjamin Franklin National Memorial* was designated as such by Congress in 1972, and was dedicated by Vice President Nelson A. Rockefeller in April of 1976. In 2008, the memorial underwent a nearly four million dollar restoration (Franklin Institute).

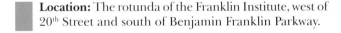

Location: The rotunda of the Franklin Institute, west of 20th Street and south of Benjamin Franklin Parkway.

Civil War Sailors and Soldiers Memorial

Completed in 1927, this marble and granite memorial by Massachusetts artist Hermon Atkins MacNeil consists of a pair of forty foot shafts flanking the Benjamin Franklin Parkway. One shaft has carved figures of sailors and the other, soldiers. The inscription atop the soldiers' pylon reads: "ONE COUNTRY / ONE CONSTITUTION / ONE DESTINY." Atop the sailors': "IN GIVING / FREEDOM TO THE SLAVE / WE ENSURE / FREEDOM TO THE FREE." The Civil War Sailors and Soldiers Memorial was meant as a gateway to the "*Parkway Gardens*," with the Art Museum as the point of anchor, so to speak (FPAA).

The *Civil War Sailors and Soldiers Memorial* was a departure from MacNeil's usual subjects, which dealt with aspects of the American West, especially Native American culture. In 1902, MacNeil received a commission for his *Coming of the White Man*, which depicts two Native Americans sternly observing the imminent European onslaught. This bronze monument was installed five years later in Washington Park in Portland, Oregon. His *A Moqui Prayer for Rain* (1896) and *The Sun Vow* (1899) are on display at the Metropolitan Museum of Art. MacNeil taught at Cornell University, and later traveled to Paris, Rome, and throughout the American West, where he observed firsthand the practices and rituals of the tribes who so inspired him.

The gateway to the "*Parkway Gardens.*" Photo courtesy of Peter J. Obst.

Location: North and south sides of Benjamin Franklin Parkway, west of 20th Street.

Diego de Gardoqui

France was undoubtedly America's biggest ally in the struggle for independence against Great Britain, a gesture which, ironically, seriously depleted France's coffers and contributed to the discontent that spawned the French Revolution. But France had ulterior motives in aiding the colonial cause, the foremost of which was revenge for a French defeat in the Seven Years War. England's other neighbors had a vested interest in weakening the British Empire, too. Among those countries was Spain, which had also butted heads with the British, most memorably in 1588 (the year of the Spanish Armada). In addition, Spain held a large amount of territory in America. So when the American Revolution erupted, Spain "endorsed" the colonies. The Spanish king sent his envoy, Diego de Gardoqui (1735–1798), and with him money, and winter blankets for the frozen troops at Valley Forge. This statue of Gardoqui, sculpted by Spaniard Antonio Sanguin, was a gift from Spain's King Juan Carlos I in 1977.

Location: East side of Logan Square, west of 18th Street and north of the Benjamin Franklin Parkway.

Diego de Gardoqui. Photo courtesy of Stan Horwitz.

General Francisco de Miranda

Dedicated in 1977, this dramatic statue of Venezuelan general Francisco de Miranda is a copy of a 1920s original by sculptor Lorenzo Gonzalez. Gonzalez's statue is located in France, at the site of a 1792 battle between French and Prussian forces that ended with a decisive French victory.

Miranda fought alongside "the Liberator," Simon de Bolivar, in the early years of the nineteenth century for Venezuelan independence from Spain, although the process was a protracted one and the victory somewhat incomplete. Prior to that, Miranda lent his military talents to the cause of American independence and, for that reason, he is memorialized in Philadelphia.

Location: 20th and Winter streets and Benjamin Franklin Parkway.

General Francisco de Miranda, 1977, by Lorenzo Gonzalez. *Photo courtesy of Tatiana Heller.*

General Galusha Pennypacker

Charles Grafly's tendency toward abstruse symbolism (Bach: 64) is evident in the 1934 memorial to General Galusha Pennypacker. The towering bronze figure depicted is not Pennypacker, but a bare-chested Roman soldier standing in a chariot flanked by a pair of tigers. The tiger on the right is poised but contained, while the beast on the left bares his fangs in a silent snarl. The inscription on the granite base reads: "GALUSHA PENNYPACKER / BREVET MAJOR GENERAL / UNITED STATES ARMY / 1844-1916." (The term "brevet" refers to a promotion in rank without the accompanying pay raise.) Viewers can glean virtually no information about the subject, who was both a Medal of Honor recipient and the Union Army's youngest general. Grafly designed the Pennypacker memorial, but died five years prior to its installation. Albert Laessle, a former student of Grafly's at the Pennsylvania Academy of Fine Arts, took over after Grafly's death. Laessle was known for animal sculptures, the most famous of which is his *Billy* (1914), the bronze goat at 19th and Locust streets in Rittenhouse Square.

Pennypacker was born in Chester County, Pennsylvania, in 1844. At age sixteen, he joined the Civil War effort, and within a year was a captain in the 97th Pennsylvania Volunteer Regiment. In January of 1865, then Colonel Pennypacker led a charge against the enemy's stronghold of Fort Fisher, in North Carolina. Just as Pennypacker placed his regiment's flag on the opposing parapet, he took a bullet in the side. As he had no less than eight or nine times throughout numerous battles during the Civil War, Pennypacker survived his injury, but just barely this time. Two months after the war ended, he was promoted to brigadier general at age twenty. In 1891, Pennypacker was awarded the Medal of Honor for his bravery at Fort Fisher.

Location: North side of Logan Square, Benjamin Franklin Parkway east of 19th Street.

The *General Galusha Pennypacker Memorial*, not an exact representation of the subject! *Photo courtesy of Stan Horwitz.*

General Tadeusz Kosciuszko

During the American Revolution, the thirty-year-old Kosciuszko came to America and introduced himself to Benjamin Franklin, who tasked the Polish engineer with designing and building forts. Kosciuszko was soon made chief engineer of the Continental Army, fortifying American defenses at Saratoga and West Point, New York. He served with both generals Horatio Gates and Nathanael Greene in the northern and southern armies, respectively (Poles in America Foundation, Inc). Kosciuszko gave all the money that he earned as a general in the Revolutionary War to his good friend, Thomas Jefferson, instructing the future U.S. president to buy as many slaves as he could, free those slaves, and provide them with land and the equipment to work that land. Jefferson never did this, however (FPAA). Kosciuszko returned to Poland in 1794 to secure his country's independence from Russia. He was unsuccessful in this endeavor, and Poland was partitioned between Russia and Prussia. Kosciuszko was imprisoned for two years in Russia, released, and returned briefly to the United States before embarking for his homeland once more in 1798. He died in Switzerland in 1817 at the age of seventy-one.

Marian Konieczny's sculpture, installed in 1979, depicts Kosciuszko in full uniform, his right hand behind his back, clutching scrolled construction plans. A sheathed sword hangs at his left flank. The *Kosciuszko* statue is across the street from Kopernik, the memorial to Polish astronomer Nicolaus Copernicus. The Philadelphia house at 3rd and Pine streets where Kosciuszko resided for five months has been preserved as a museum by the National Park Service.

Location: Southwest corner of 18th Street and Benjamin Franklin Parkway, across the street from Kopernik.

General Tadeusz Kosciuszko, by Marian Konieczny. *Photo courtesy of Peter J. Obst.*

Joseph Leidy

For twenty-two years, the *Leidy Memorial* stood at City Hall. *Photo courtesy of Tatiana Heller.*

Since 1929, the statue of world-renowned scientist and Philadelphia native Joseph Leidy (1832–1891) has stood in front of the Academy of Natural Sciences, an appropriate venue for a memorial to a man who was both a founding member of that venerable institution and served as its president. Created by fellow Philadelphian Samuel Murray, the sculpture was first placed on the west plaza of City Hall, and dedicated on Wednesday, October 30, 1907. Leidy's accomplishments and contributions to multiple branches of science are too numerous to list on the statue's pedestal, which bears only his name and the years of his life.

Titles such as "the Father of American Vertebrate Paleontology" and "the Founder of American Parasitology" have been bestowed upon Leidy, who was posthumously dubbed "the last man who knew everything" by a biographer (Academy of Natural Sciences). Leidy was trained as a medical doctor, receiving his degree from the University of Pennsylvania in 1844. During the brief time that he practiced medicine, he discovered the parasite in pork that causes trichinosis, and recommended thoroughly cooking the meat to prevent the disease. Leidy later did pioneering research on parasites in termites.

Although the categorization is very limiting considering the scope of Leidy's activities, he is primarily remembered for his work in paleontology. He amassed hundreds of fossils from the American West, poring over the specimens in his study at the Academy of Natural Sciences. After examining the bones of the large herbivorous dinosaur Hadrosaurus, Leidy concluded that the creature walked on two legs, not on four as a leading paleontologist of the day had previously stated. Leidy's interests in the natural world extended to geology and mineralogy, and he eventually donated his extensive gem collection to the Smithsonian Institution.

Leidy taught at the University of Pennsylvania and Swarthmore College, and gave a series of lectures at the former that proved extremely popular. He was also president of the Wagner Free Institute of Science. An avid author and illustrator, Leidy published hundreds of essays, pamphlets, and articles detailing his findings, and also authored numerous books. He died in Philadelphia in 1891 at the age of sixty-seven.

Location: In front of the Academy of Natural Sciences, 19th and Race streets and the Benjamin Franklin Parkway.

Kopernik

Designed by artist Dudley V. Talcott, this steel and red granite structure was dedicated in 1973 to commemorate the 500th anniversary of the birth of Polish astronomer Nicolaus Copernicus (1473–1543). The metal portion at the top of this twenty-four foot tall memorial is intended to symbolize the earth revolving around the sun, and the granite base and plinth are meant to resemble a telescope. Behind the memorial, on the left and right respectively, are the flags of the United States and Poland. *Kopernik* was sponsored by the Polish Heritage Society. The sculptor was also the author of three novels.

For centuries, the assertion by second-century Egyptian scientist Ptolemy (c. 100–170 A.D.) that the sun and the other planets revolved around the earth was accepted by both the scientific and religious communities. In fact, suggesting otherwise was tantamount to heresy according to the Church, and later Copernican proponents were persecuted. Monk Giordano Bruno (1548–1600) was burned at the stake by the Inquisition, and Galileo Galilei (1564–1642), while not physically harmed, was placed under house arrest and forced to recant. While studying in Italy, following his graduation from the University of Cracow, Copernicus further cultivated his burgeoning interest in astronomy, primarily as a means of establishing a more accurate calendar (Gale). Many years of mathematical formulae and assiduous celestial observations preceded his official findings, but even after his first paper on the heliocentric solar system in 1514, his theories were not widely-circulated outside of the scientific community. Copernicus died in Frauenberg, Poland, in 1543 at the age of seventy, shortly after the publication of his book *De Revolutionibus Orbium Coelestium* (*Revolutions of the Heavenly Spheres*).

Location: Between Benjamin Franklin Parkway and Race Street, east of 18th Street, across the street from the *General Tadeusz Kosciuszko* memorial.

Two birds find a haven at the apogee of *Kopernik*. Photo courtesy of Peter J. Obst.

Monument to the Six Million Jewish Martyrs/ Philadelphia Holocaust Memorial

Dedicated on April 26, 1964, this monument by the late Nathan Rapoport commemorates one of history's most heinous massacres, the slaughter of two-thirds of European Jewry during the Second World War. The four-and-a-half foot granite base supports a writhing, fourteen foot bronze sculpture group that twists mournfully toward the sky. Flames are the central motif, and within the fire are figures of a woman, a child, and a man. About halfway to the top of the sculpture, disembodied hands protruding from the conflagration clutch a Torah. Farther up, two more hands brandish short swords, symbolizing the Jewish resistance to the Nazis. One of the inscriptions, on the right side of the base, lists the concentration camps where six million Jews—and five million non-Jews—perished during the Holocaust. Annual ceremonies mark the anniversary of the monument's dedication. Also known as the Philadelphia Holocaust Memorial, the work was sponsored by the Association of Jewish New Americans.

Antisemitism was not new to Europe or the rest of the world when Adolf Hitler came to power in 1933. Jews had been persecuted since ancient times, and the Fuhrer viewed them as the perfect scapegoats for Germany's social and economic troubles in the wake of the First World War. Jews were systematically stripped of their rights, forced into ghettos, and then shipped off to labor camps, where those who were too sick, too old or too young to work were killed. With the Nazis' "Final Solution" in 1942, the emphasis shifted from forced labor to outright slaughter. The most infamous of the camps was Auschwitz in Poland, where about three million died, many in the gas chambers. In addition to Jews, the Nazis slaughtered Gypsies, homosexuals, Jehovah's Witnesses, the handicapped, and political dissidents.

Location: 16th and Arch streets and Benjamin Franklin Parkway.

Dedicated in 1964, Nathan Rapoport's disturbing memorial commemorates one of history's darkest chapters.
Photo courtesy of Tatiana Heller.

Shakespeare Memorial

In Alexander Stirling Calder's sculpture, the two contrasting themes of comedy and tragedy are represented by Hamlet, the ill-fated prince of Denmark, and Touchstone the Jester, from *As You Like It*. The lugubrious prince is clutching a dagger and contemplating self-destruction, while the frivolous jester beside him is laughing. Perhaps the most famous quote from Shakespeare's aforementioned comedy is inscribed on the front of the fourteen foot black granite pedestal: "All the world's a stage, and all the men and women merely players (Act 2, scene 7, 139-140)."

Stirling Calder received the commission for the *Shakespeare Memorial* in 1917, and the work was unveiled on April 23, 1929, the 365th anniversary of the Bard's birth. The pair of figures was cast by Roman Bronze Works of New York. In 1953, the memorial was moved to accommodate construction of the Schuylkill Expressway.

Actor turned playwright William Shakespeare (1564–1616) has been lauded as the quintessential English dramatist for both his skillful use of language and his keen insight into the human psyche. Still, there are those less enthusiastic readers who find his works dated and inaccessible to modern readers. Early in his career he was successful enough to elicit the jealousy of writer Robert Greene, who resentfully labeled Shakespeare as "an upstart crow, beautified with our feathers (Abrams: 866)." Most of his thirty-seven plays—divided into comedies, tragedies, and histories—were written over a twenty-year period. A prolific poet as well, Shakespeare penned 154 sonnets, which were published in 1609. Seven years after his death, two actors from his old theater company, The King's Men, collected and published the first comprehensive collection of his plays, *The First Folio*. Debate has arisen over the years whether Shakespeare—who did not possess an extensive formal education—really wrote the plays attributed to him, but skeptics have offered little concrete proof.

Location: North side of Logan Square, 19th Street and Benjamin Franklin Parkway, across from Free Library.

The Bard's memorial is aptly represented by tragedy and comedy.

Swann Memorial Fountain

That Philadelphia sculptor Alexander Stirling Calder intended an eponymous pun when he paired two of his reclining bronze figures—the *Schuylkill* and the *Wissahickon*—with large swans, is not beyond the realm of possibility. But regardless of this, the significance of these majestic waterfowl is evident in a statuary group representing Pennsylvania rivers. Given that the *Schuylkill* and the *Wissahickon* are depicted as female, bonding them to lithe, graceful birds seems natural, although the poses of the two women, as well as that of the two birds, are starkly different. The *Schuylkill* appears to be throttling her swan, and the animal's wings are perpendicular to its body, indicating a struggle. The *Wissahickon* lies on her left side, and while her swan's posture is erect, the bird is not in any evident distress. Represented by a male Indian figure, the languid *Delaware* leans against a large fish, possibly a bass, creating a contrast between his two distaff counterparts while remaining congruent with the fountain's motif. Alternating frogs and turtles encircle the three central pieces at approximately two-thirds of the pool's radius. Quoted in a November 17, 1924, newspaper article, Calder downplayed the symbolism of the minor sculptures (Wainwright: 234).

A collaborative effort between Calder and architect Wilson Eyre, Jr., the *Swann Memorial Fountain* was officially opened on July 23, 1924, and is dedicated to Dr. Wilson Cary Swann (1806–1876), a Virginia-born physician who founded the Fountain Society of Philadelphia in 1869. During its fifty-five-year existence, the society erected and maintained many public drinking fountains in the city of Philadelphia. The purpose of these watering spots was to quench the thirst of both people and animals and to discourage the consumption of alcohol by providing a more salubrious alternative. Swann's wife, Maria, bequeathed $50,000 to build a memorial fountain for her late husband. Maria died in 1891, but work on the memorial did not commence until twenty-six years later, with the appointment of Eyre to design the project. In 1921, Calder was contracted to create the bronze sculptures. Of the fountain's three central sculptures, the *Wissahickon* was completed first, followed by the *Delaware*, and finally the *Schuylkill*.

Location: Logan Circle, 19th Street and Benjamin Franklin Parkway.

The *Swann Memorial Fountain* on a hot summer day.

And on a cool winter day. *Photo courtesy of Peter J. Obst*.

The Ideal Boy Scout

The concept for this six foot, quarter-ton bronze statue came about many years before its official dedication on June 12, 1937. Ten limited edition models, about one-and-a-half feet tall, were first produced, each of them selling for one hundred dollars. Sculptor R. Tait McKenzie modeled his original 1914 design after a young Boy Scout with the lengthy name of Asa Franklin Williamson Hooven. The larger piece, which stands at Boy Scout Headquarters in Philadelphia, is an amalgamation of several youths' features, and was commissioned sixteen years later when the Scouts moved from their 9th and Walnut streets location into their current building (BSA).

 Location: Boy Scout Headquarters, southeast corner of 22nd and Winter streets.

A model of the statue that stands in front of the Boy Scout Headquarters on 22nd and Winter streets in Philadelphia. *Photo courtesy of Boy Scouts of America, Cradle of Liberty Council.*

Bridesburg 3

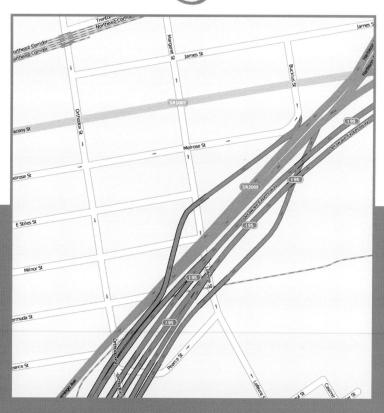

Peace Memorial

Harold Kimmelman possesses an obvious talent for bending ostensibly intractable media into forms beautiful, bizarre—or in the opinion of some—grotesque. Kimmelman has described his efforts as essentially infusing life into metal, his preferred material being steel. This 1974 installation is fairly straightforward; even without the accompanying inscription, the United States flag and the emblems of the four major branches of service indicate that the work is a tribute to the men and women of our armed forces. Other commissions are less apparent, and arguably subjected to multiple interpretations. His *Decline and Rise* (1969), in West Philadelphia, consisting of a line of tumbling and standing steel beams may not necessarily suggest to the viewer the cycle of urban collapse and renewal that the artist has explained that it does (Wainwright: 328). Juxtaposed with that example are sculptures like his *Kangaroos* (1970), in Society Hill, which patently portrays a pair of frolicking marsupials. Philadelphia boasts more than a score of sculptures by Kimmelman.

Location: Near intersection of Aramingo Avenue, Margaret, and Milnor streets, beneath the Interstate 95 ramp.

The *Peace Memorial*, 1974 by Harold Kimmelman. *Photo courtesy of Stan Horwitz.*

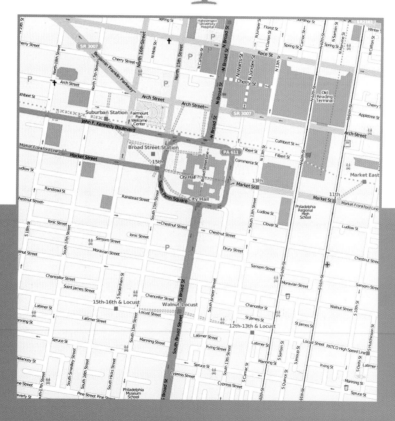

Benjamin Franklin – Craftsman

Dedicated on June 27, 1981, this bronze monument, intended to commemorate the 250th anniversary of Pennsylvania Freemasons, depicts a young Benjamin Franklin operating a printing press. The front of the platform on which the sculpture rests reads, "BENJAMIN FRANKLIN – CRAFTSMAN." The sculptor was Joseph Brown of Princeton, New Jersey.

As industrious as he was intellectual, Franklin was the rare sort of person who excelled at numerous pursuits. He is remembered as a patriot, statesman, diplomat, linguist, scientist, inventor, and writer. But his first vocation was as a printer, apprenticed at twelve to his older brother. Literarily inclined from an early age, Franklin went on to own and operate a newspaper, *The Pennsylvania Gazette*, and publish his witty, didactic magazine *Poor Richard's Almanack*. Although a man of exceptional intelligence, Franklin maintained an unpretentious, down-to-earth demeanor (Baym: 360).

Franklin traveled extensively back and forth to Europe, and spent the American Revolution abroad in France—where he was held in the highest regard—garnering allies and assets for his country's struggle for independence. In his travels to England prior to the war, Franklin grew convinced that the mother country was out of touch with her colonies. Franklin's son William, who served as governor of New Jersey, was a Tory, and this led to an irreparable schism between the two.

During a 1774 visit to London, Franklin was lambasted by British officials for leaking information about correspondence written by Thomas Hutchinson, the royal governor of Massachusetts. Hutchinson's letters were critical of Britain's treatment of the colonies. (In fact, Samuel Adams, propagandist and agitator extraordinaire, had been responsible for the breach.) This was a turning point for Franklin, who realized then that reconciliation with England was impossible (Greystone Communications). At the Treaty of Paris in 1783, which officially ended the Revolutionary War, Franklin served as the American delegate. He died in Philadelphia in 1790, and is interred in Christ Church Burial Ground with his wife, Deborah.

Location: Northwest corner of Broad Street and John F. Kennedy Boulevard.

SMAN

Far left:
One of many city memorials to Benjamin Franklin (who was actually from Boston). *Photo courtesy of Tatiana Heller.*

Left:
A side view of Ben. *Photo courtesy of Tatiana Heller.*

Clothespin

Born in Stockholm, Sweden, in 1929, Claes Oldenburg is known for creating the quirky, out of the mundane. In particular, Oldenburg takes ordinary items like hamburgers or flashlights or baseball bats and turns them into oversized, outrageous *objets d'art*. His forty-five foot steel *Clothespin*—installed at 15th and Markets streets in 1976—is a prime example. While the opinion on its aesthetic quality is mixed, no one can argue that its impact is arresting, even startling. Oldenburg has suggested that his enormous opus represents something different to every viewer. He admitted that he drew part of his inspiration from the monolithic minimalist sculpture *The Kiss* (1908), by Romanian sculptor Constantin Brancusi. *Clothespin* was funded by the city Redevelopment Authority's One Percent Program. Established in 1959 by a bill from former city councilman Henry Sawyer, the program mandated that one percent of a building's construction cost be allotted for an accompanying piece of artwork. *Clothespin* was part of the budget for developer Jack Wolgin's $80 million Centre Square, with enough left over for several other works of art (Hine).

Oldenburg and his wife, Coosje van Bruggen, have collaborated on a number of projects, among them *Split Button*, on the campus of the University of Pennsylvania. Installed in 1981, the piece is pretty much exactly what the name says: a large button with a split, slightly to the right of center. Oldenburg's work can also be seen in Chicago and Las Vegas.

Location: Centre Square, 15th and Market streets.

Claes Oldenburg's *Clothespin*. Either you love it ... or you don't. *Photo courtesy of Tatiana Heller.*

Emancipation Proclamation Fountain

The so-called *Emancipation Proclamation Fountain* has not functioned as an active conduit for water for many years, but still stands in the subway concourse at 15th and Market streets. Any architectural vestiges of a fountain are long since gone. In the warmer months, the bronze sculpture atop its concrete base is largely obscured by leafy boughs from surrounding trees. But closer inspection, which requires descending the steps, reveals an eight foot abstract figure of a woman. From the hand of her outstretched left arm sprouts a trio of doves, ostensibly being set free. Completed in 1964 and dedicated February 12 of the following year, the piece was commissioned by the city of Philadelphia to mark the 100th anniversary of Abraham Lincoln's historic decree. Funded by pennies donated by school children, the sculpture was cast at the Bedi-Rassy Art Foundry in New York.

More than anything else, the Emancipation Proclamation earned President Lincoln the title of "Great Emancipator." At the time of its issuance, however—January 1, 1863—the nation was still in the midst of a bloody civil war. Enforcement of the proclamation was contingent on a Union victory, which was by no means a foregone conclusion. The completion, if not the actual dedication of the *Emancipation Proclamation Fountain*, coincided with the passage of the Civil Rights Act of 1964. This likely gave the event additional significance.

Sculptor Gerd Utescher was born in Germany in 1912 and emigrated to the United States in 1949. He created several other pieces in Philadelphia, all of which feature abstract representations of the human form, combined with appropriate symbolism for the respective subjects. He taught at several institutions, including the Philadelphia College of Art and the Pennsylvania Academy of the Fine Arts. The seventy-one-year-old Utescher died in Genoa, Italy, in

The *Emancipation Proclamation Fountain*, located in the Penn Center subway concourse, 15th and Market streets, and long since dry. *Photo courtesy of Tatiana Heller.*

April of 1983, from injuries sustained after a freak accident in which a load of bricks fell on him.

Location: Penn Center subway concourse, 15th and Market streets.

Frank L. Rizzo

Unveiled on New Years Day of 1999, this 10-foot, one-ton bronze of former Philadelphia mayor Frank L. Rizzo was created by Glenside, Pennsylvania, sculptor Zenos Frudakis. Nicknamed "the Big Bambino," Rizzo served two consecutive terms in office, from 1972 to 1980. In 1988 he ran unsuccessfully for a third term against Democrat W. Wilson Goode. Rizzo died of a heart attack in July of 1991, while again campaigning—this time for the Republican mayoral nomination against former District Attorney Ronald D. Castille. Joseph M. Egan, Jr. wound up with the party's endorsement following Rizzo's death, but lost to Democrat Edward G. Rendell. Prior to being Philadelphia's mayor, Rizzo was the city's police commissioner from 1967 to 1971, after having been on the force for twenty-four years. To his supporters, Rizzo, the top cop, was a no-nonsense crime-fighter who cracked down hard on miscreants. To critics, he was over-zealous and even brutal, especially toward minorities. But regardless of what anyone thought about Rizzo, he was undeniably a potent force in Philadelphia politics for many years.

The *Frank L. Rizzo Monument* Committee, consisting of family and friends of the former mayor, was formed in 1992. Frudakis, who was commissioned in 1994, received $100,000 for the Rizzo statue, which was modeled from a photograph taken of Rizzo at a 1972 Saint Patrick's Day parade. Mayor Rizzo faces the north side of City Hall, and is depicted descending the steps, while waving with his right hand. He is dressed in a suit and tie. Frudakis did not want the bronze Rizzo put on a pedestal, citing Rizzo's status as a man of the people. The statue, which was cast at a foundry in Chester, Pennsylvania, took Frudakis five years to complete, during which time the sculptor interviewed those closest to Rizzo, studied other photographs, and even tried on the late mayor's shoes.

The January 1 dedication of the Rizzo monument drew a small crowd of between 100 and 200, including Rizzo's son, Frank Jr., widow, Carmella, brother, Joseph, and daughter, Joanna Mastronardo, as well as other family members and former political associates. In his speech, Mayor Rendell indicated that the Municipal Services Building was the perfect place for a statue of Rizzo. Also in attendance were future mayor John F. Street and Rizzo's campaign manager, Marty Weinberg.

On the steps of the Municipal Services Building, a nine foot bronze Frank Rizzo waves at passers-by. *Photo courtesy of Tatiana Heller.*

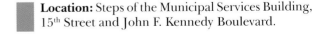

Location: Steps of the Municipal Services Building, 15th Street and John F. Kennedy Boulevard.

General George B. McClellan

The young George B. McClellan showed great promise as a soldier, graduating second in his class at West Point and being thrice promoted during the Mexican War (1846–1848). He later taught at his alma mater before working for two railroads, the first as an engineer and the second as its president (Wooster: 25). His Civil War commands began with Department of the Ohio volunteers and ended with the Army of the Potomac. Historians agree that "Little Mac's" greatest liability was his reluctance to fully commit his troops in the field, which led to the alternate sobriquet "Mac the Unready" (Shotgun). While his contemporary Ulysses S. Grant did not hesitate to send thousands of young men to their deaths in order to ensure a Union victory, McClellan was reluctant to take advantage of favorable positions and superior numbers. This led to his being relieved of command of the Army of the Potomac and replaced by Ambrose Burnside in November of 1862, after having held the post for thirteen months.

In 1864, McClellan ran on the Democratic ticket against the Republican Lincoln, who soundly defeated him. He later had to content himself with serving as governor of New Jersey, an office which he occupied twice. McClellan died in 1885 in Orange, New Jersey, a few months after Ulysses S. Grant.

Plans to erect a memorial to the native Philadelphian were made shortly after his death, by a fifteen-member committee appointed by Mayor William Smith to represent Philadelphia at the general's funeral. Original designs calling for a standing figure of McClellan were later changed to those for an equestrian statue. This and other delays resulted in the pedestal sitting vacant for three years. Henry Jackson Ellicott's sculpture was finally unveiled in 1894. The McClellan memorial was sponsored by the Grand Army of the Republic, a once very-influential organization founded by Union Civil War veterans.

Location: Broad Street and John F. Kennedy Boulevard, north side of City Hall.

General George B. McClellan by Henry Jackson Ellicott. *Photo courtesy of Tatiana Heller.*

General John Fulton Reynolds

Like several other Civil War generals on both sides of the conflict, John Fulton Reynolds was a West Point graduate and Mexican War veteran. A battle-hardened soldier, he was accustomed to both taking and giving orders, but was overruled by President Lincoln after specifying certain stipulations under which he would accept command of the Army of the Potomac prior to the Battle of Gettysburg (July 1–July 3, 1863). He was therefore passed over in favor of George Gordon Meade, and instead given command of the 1st, 3rd, and 11th Corps—which comprised the left wing—of the Army of the Potomac. But Gettysburg was to be his last battle; the brave Reynolds was felled by a Rebel bullet. When the bloody confrontation was over, combined Northern and Southern casualties exceeded 40,000. Confederate General Robert E. Lee's bold incursion into Union territory had failed to force a Union surrender, and the war would drag on for nearly two more years.

Twenty-one years later, the city of Philadelphia dedicated an equestrian statue of the slain Reynolds. The general is depicted pointing toward the enemy, while his steed paws the ground nervously. The detail and expression on the faces of both horse and rider are painfully realistic. Cast at a local foundry, this twelve-foot, 7,000-pound bronze work sits atop a ten-foot granite pedestal. Sculptor John Rogers worked out of his Connecticut studio. The Reynolds memorial was both the city's first equestrian statue, and the first monument to a Civil War general.

Location: Broad Street and John F. Kennedy Boulevard, north side of City Hall.

Sculptor John Rogers captured General John Fulton Reynolds and his horse in a dramatic pose. *Photo courtesy of Tatiana Heller.*

The other side of Rogers' Reynolds. *Photo courtesy of Tatiana Heller.*

George Washington

This bronze Washington was actually cast in 1908, and was based on an 1869 marble original, which today resides inside of City Hall. The artist, Joseph A. Bailly, was a French wood carver who came to the United States in 1850. Among Bailly's commissions were monuments for Philadelphia's famous Laurel Hill Cemetery, a statue of Benjamin Franklin inside the Public Ledger building on 6th and Chestnut streets, and a statue of Reverend John Witherspoon at the Horticultural Center at Belmont Avenue and Montgomery Drive.

Location: In front of Independence Hall, south side of Chestnut Street between 5th and 6th streets.

This bronze Washington was actually cast in 1908, and was based on an 1869 marble original, which today resides inside of City Hall. *Photo courtesy of Vlad Ringe.*

Government of the People

Installed in 1976, this sculpture looks to some like a grotesque, distorted pile of humanity. One of its figures resembles a female Atlas with stocky, stone arms outstretched, and ossified breasts salient. At the top is a roughly vertical structure, like a stone set with numerous grooves and indentations. Philadelphia Mayor Frank L. Rizzo considered the work of dubious artistic quality, and refused to appropriate city funds for its installation. The mayor's infamous remark about the sculpture was that "it looked like a plasterer dropped a load of plaster." The piece was not installed until three years after sculptor Jacques Lipchitz's death. Lipchitz's other works in Philadelphia include *Prometheus Strangling the Vulture*, in front of the Art Museum, and the *Spirit of Enterprise*, part of the Ellen Phillips Samuel Memorial on Kelly Drive.

Born in Lithuania in 1891, Lipchitz studied at the Ecole des Beaux-Arts and the Academie Julian in Paris while a young man. During his time in France he hobnobbed with various artists, among them Pablo Picasso, who profoundly influenced his sculptural style. Lipchitz, who was Jewish, managed to flee Nazi-occupied France during the Second World War. He and his wife settled in the United States in 1941, residing in New York until his death, with the exception of a 1946 return trip to France. A number of his works in the wake of his exodus from Europe dealt with the themes of war, loss, and destruction (Wilkinson). His autobiography—*My Life in Sculpture*—was published in 1972.

Location: Plaza of the Municipal Services Building, northwest corner of Broad Street and John F. Kennedy Boulevard.

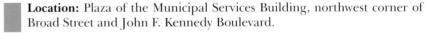

Jacques Lipchitz's *Government of the People*. Photo courtesy of Peter J. Obst.

John Christian Bullitt

John J. Boyle's heroic bronze of lawyer and businessman John Christian Bullitt was installed in 1907, a mere five years after the subject's death, remarkably fast considering monuments of similar scale have sat on the drawing table for decades. The Bullitt statue, which rises fifteen feet in the air from the bottom of the granite pedestal to the top of Bullitt's head, was funded through private donations. Bullitt was a strong supporter of construction of the Benjamin Franklin Parkway, a thoroughfare that most Philadelphians take for granted, although he didn't live long enough to see the road's completion. Among Bullitt's contributions to city government was a bill that consolidated municipal departments and gave more power to the mayor (Brenner: 15).

Location: North side of City Hall, Broad Street and John F. Kennedy Boulevard.

John Christian Bullitt, 1907 by John J. Boyle. *Photo courtesy of Tatiana Heller.*

John Wanamaker, Citizen

Sculptor John Massey Rhind intended to make his 1923 statue of John Wanamaker unpretentious. He said of the piece:

> I couldn't do a "stagey" portrait of such a man, even if I wanted to. As he stands there, he is both at rest and in action. I have tried to show him just ready to walk out of his office and stopping to say, "Well, how big of an order shall we place for those goods today?" (McSpadden: 261)

Philadelphian John Wanamaker (1838–1922) might be called the father of the department store. Before founding the retail establishment in 1876 that became an empire, Wanamaker ran a haberdashery with his brother-in-law, Nathan Brown. Wanamaker implemented a number of business practices that seemed almost radical at the time, but today are standard protocol, like fixed prices for certain items instead of haggling, and money back guarantees. As a result, customers trusted Wanamaker, and kept coming back (PBS). In 1889, President Benjamin Harrison (1889–1893) appointed Wanamaker Postmaster General. Wanamaker died on December 12, 1922.

Born in Edinburgh, Scotland, in 1860, Rhind immigrated to the United States in 1889 with his new bride. The son and grandson of sculptors, he received training at home, and studied in both England and France. Upon arriving in America, Rhind set up shop on 20th Street in New York City. The assiduous young artist won a competition sponsored by John Jacob Astor to design one of three bronze door panels for Trinity Church. Rhind's panel depicted the expulsion of Adam and Eve from the Garden of Eden. Architectural embellishments comprised a large part of Rhind's career, but he was always adamant that sculptural adornments not overshadow the architecture (McSpadden: 254-258). Rhind also created massive memorials, like the one to slain President William McKinley in McKinley's hometown of Niles, Ohio, and that of South Carolina politician John C. Calhoun in Charleston.

Location: East side of City Hall, Juniper and Market streets.

John Wanamaker, Citizen, 1923 by John Massey Rhind. *Photo courtesy of Tatiana Heller.*

Love Sculpture

This unique, universally-recognized arrangement of the letters in the word "love" was extrapolated from a 1964 painting by Robert Indiana. In 1976, Indiana's Love sculpture was installed at its current location, at John F. Kennedy Plaza, popularly known as Love Park. After attempts to sell the sculpture in New York City failed, the chairman of the Philadelphia Art Commission purchased the piece for his city (FPAA). Indiana's iconic design has been replicated on t-shirts, jewelry, coffee cups, prints, silk screens, and tattoos. In 1973, the United States Post Office issued a commemorative eight-cent *Love* stamp, which proved extremely popular. "The great innovation was this tilting of the letter O onto this diagonal," said writer Adrian Dannatt. "It is this diagonal that turns the word into [...] a perfect square" (ibid.). Another interesting geometric phenomenon occurs, due to the placement of the L directly over the V: an inverted spades symbol, like that found on a suit of playing cards, is formed.

Born in 1928, pop artist guru and sometime activist Robert Indiana changed his surname from Clark to that of his home state in his thirtieth year. Outwardly committed to starting a trend away from abstract art, he nevertheless produced a series of sculptures in the early 1960s that were basically composed of neighborhood junk. Most Americans under the age of fifty probably do not even know the name of Robert Indiana, and those who do will almost invariably associate him solely with the *Love* sculpture. Indiana is also a painter, poet, author, theater set and costume designer, and has occasionally collaborated with other artists, among them the late Andy Warhol. Indiana has resided in Vinalhaven, Maine, since 1978.

Location: John F. Kennedy Plaza (Love Park), 15th Street and John F. Kennedy Boulevard, and also Locust Walk and 36th Street.

A couple poses underneath Robert Indiana's famous *Love* sculpture. *Photo courtesy of Tatiana Heller.*

Mary Dyer

The original of this 1959 sculpture by Sylvia Shaw Judson is in front of the State House in Boston, where the piece was commissioned by an ancestor of the martyred Quaker, Mary Dyer (1611–1660), who was executed for her religious beliefs. A replica of Judson's statue was installed at the Friends Center in Philadelphia in 1975. Depicting a seated Mary Dyer with her hands folded neatly on her lap, the work suggests modesty and quiet courage. The inscription reads: "Quaker witness for religious freedom. Hanged on Boston Common 1660."

Little is known of Dyer's life prior to her and her husband William's arrival in Boston from England in 1635, but credible research conducted by a descendant strongly suggests that she was the daughter of Arabella Stuart—a cousin of England's King James I—and Sir William Seymour (Plimpton: 13). Mary clashed with the Puritan leaders of Boston when she befriended Ann Hutchinson, whose different religious views resulted in her exile. The Dyers and others with similar sympathies moved to Rhode Island to escape the intolerance that they found in Boston. Mary and William were not Quakers at that point: not until several years later—during a return visit to England—did they meet Quaker founder George Fox, and convert. In 1658, draconian laws targeting Quakers were passed in Boston.

Mary could have remained permanently in Rhode Island and not looked back, but when her fellow Quakers Marmaduke Stevenson and William Robinson were jailed in Boston in 1659, she visited them. She was thrown in jail herself, but she and her friends were released on the stipulation that they not return. In an act of peaceful defiance, the trio did come back to Boston, an act that cost Stevenson and Robinson their lives, and nearly cost Mary the same but for a last-minute reprieve from the governor of Massachusetts. But Mary would be neither banished nor intimidated: she returned to Boston a final time in 1660 to profess her beliefs and protest the injustices perpetrated on Quakers. She went unwavering to the gallows on June 1.

■ **Location:** Friends Center, 15th and Cherry streets.

Mary Dyer (1611–1660), Quaker martyr. Photo courtesy of J. Bady, Friends Center.

Matthias William Baldwin

Like Stephen Girard (1750–1831), Matthias William Baldwin (1795–1886) was as much a philanthropist as a tycoon, donating regularly and generously to various charities and institutions. Among the latter was the Franklin Institute. In the 1830s he founded Baldwin Locomotive works, the largest locomotive manufacturer at the time. His most famous project was a six-ton locomotive called "Old Ironsides," completed in 1832. Old Ironsides was capable of pulling five times its weight on a flat surface at a speed of twenty-eight miles per hour (Franklin Institute).

This statue of Baldwin, by Herbert Adams, was erected in 1905 at Broad and Spring Garden streets, the site of his factory, but was relocated in 1921.

Location: North side of City Hall, Broad Street and John F. Kennedy Boulevard.

Baldwin founded Baldwin Locomotive works, the largest locomotive manufacturer at the time, the nineteenth century. (Salisbury). *Photo courtesy of Tatiana Heller.*

Otters (for William W. Bodine, Jr.)

Otters (memorial for William F. Bodine, Jr.), 1979 by Henry Mitchell. *Photo courtesy of Michael Starr, Jefferson University Hospital.*

An inscription reads, "With gratitude to William W. Bodine, Jr. Leader, builder and friend of Thomas Jefferson University." The fountain was, as the inscription hints, not originally intended as a memorial, as Bodine (1918–1983) was still alive when the piece was installed, but as a token of appreciation to the former president, and later chairman, of Thomas Jefferson University. Bodine's career also included stints in the insurance and financial management fields, interspersed with his positions at Jefferson. His leadership qualities manifested themselves in civic circles, as well, as evidenced by his chairmanship of the World Affairs Council of Philadelphia, a non-profit, grass-roots organization, and the University City Science Center.

Dedicated in 1979, this fountain was designed by Henry Mitchell, who specialized in abstract animal-themed sculptures, including *Giraffe* (1955) at a playground at Bustleton and Magee avenues, *Impala Fountain* (1964) for the Philadelphia Zoo, *Running Free* (1971), on Drexel University's campus, depicting three wild, writhing horses with exaggeratedly long necks, and his cat fountain (1973) for the Betsy Ross House at 2nd and Arch streets. A native of Canton, Ohio, Mitchell continued a long, productive association with the city of Philadelphia, following his graduation from Tyler School of Art and a study sojourn in Milan, Italy. He divided his time between the two cities, remaining active until his death in 1980 (Guinee).

Location: Thomas Jefferson University Campus, 10th and Walnut streets.

Phoenix Rising
(Memorial to Richardson Dilworth)

The impetus for this $40,000 abstract sculpture was to rectify a perceived insult by Mayor Frank L. Rizzo as much as to honor the memory of the late Mayor Richardson Dilworth. Designed by Philadelphia artist Emlen Etting, this privately-funded memorial was unveiled November 4, 1982. Mayor William J. Green was among those present, as were friends and even former political rivals of Dilworth. Etting, who died in 1993 at the age of eighty-seven, was also a noted painter and poet who translated verse from French, and taught art at several different universities.

Dilworth, who died in 1974, was mayor of Philadelphia from 1955 to 1962, resigning in his second term to run for governor. But his second gubernatorial bid, like his first one in 1950, was unsuccessful, and he lost to Republican William W. Scranton. Dilworth and Rizzo thoroughly disliked each other, and Rizzo's critics accused him of sabotaging the July 1977 dedication of the newly-constructed plaza named for his rival by not notifying Dilworth's friends and family of the date. Rizzo himself did not attend, and later shrugged off allegations that he had deliberately snubbed Dilworth's supporters.

Interestingly, Etting himself had a dispute with Rizzo in 1958, when several Philadelphia police officers raided Etting's Panama Street home after neighbors complained of the noise from a party. Etting wrote a letter to Mayor Dilworth, protesting the rude behavior of the responding officers. In an official report, then Captain Frank L. Rizzo maintained that the police had acted in a professional manner, but that they should have arrested Etting (Wallace).

Location: Dilworth Plaza, west side of City Hall, 15th and Market streets.

Phoenix Rising (Memorial to Richardson Dilworth), 1982 by Emlen Etting. *Photo courtesy of Tatiana Heller.*

Robert Morris

Completed in 1925 by Paul Wayland Bartlett, this bronze figure of the financier of the American Revolution was cast at a foundry in Baltimore, while the limestone base was carved in New York. Originally, the commission for the Robert Morris statue was given to Richard Brooks, who died before he could finish.

Robert Morris (1734–1806) never received the fame nor glory of a George Washington or an Anthony Wayne, but in the opinion of many historians, he played as vital a role in America's winning the Revolutionary War. Possessed of uncanny business sense, he acquired considerable wealth as a merchant in Philadelphia. He was an Englishman by birth, and an American by choice, and when hostilities with Great Britain commenced, he utilized his talents to raise money for the Continental Army. Morris personally loaned $10,000 to purchase supplies for the harried troops. His financial efforts on behalf of his adopted country continued after the war, with his drafting of a plan for the establishment of a national bank in 1781. That same year he had been appointed Superintendent of Finance.

Morris was a delegate to the Continental Congress from 1775 to 1778, a signer of the Declaration of Independence, and a delegate to the Constitutional Convention in 1787. He also served a term as Pennsylvania senator (1789–1795). Sadly, his fortunes reversed near the end of his life due to poor investments. He died on May 9, 1806, at the age of seventy-three.

Location: North side of Walnut Street between 4th and 5th streets.

Not all patriots were soldiers. Robert Morris (1734—1806) financed a large part of the Revolutionary War effort for the Colonies. Ironically, he died nearly broke. *Photo courtesy of Tatiana Heller.*

Samuel D. Gross

This 1897 sculpture by Alexander Stirling Calder was originally placed at The National Library of Medicine in Washington, D.C. However, this monument to renowned surgeon Dr. Samuel D. Gross has been at its current location for forty years. It was sponsored by the American Medical Association and the Thomas Jefferson Alumni Association, with a portion of the cost funded by Congress, as well.

Location: Thomas Jefferson University Campus, 10th and Walnut streets.

The monument was sponsored by the American Medical Association and the Thomas Jefferson Alumni Association, with a portion of the cost funded by Congress, as well. *Photo courtesy of Michael Starr, Jefferson University Hospital.*

Spirit of '61

Sculpted by Henry Kirke Bush-Brown, this nine-foot monument was commissioned in 1911 to mark the fiftieth anniversary of the Pennsylvania National Guard's First Infantry Unit, called into action at the start of the Civil War. The name *Spirit of '61* of course refers to the year 1861. Bush-Brown's sculpture is appropriately paired with J. Wilson's Washington Grays Monument, from which the Guard's First Infantry Unit originated. (See the following entry). The plaque on the granite pedestal reads: "First Regiment Infantry / National Guard / of / Pennsylvania / (Gray Reserves) / 1861–April 19–1911." The Civil War started on 19 April 1861.

Location: In front of the Union League, southwest corner of Broad and Sansom streets.

The *Spirit of '61*, by Henry Kirke Bush-Brown. *Photo courtesy of Tatiana Heller.*

Washington Grays Monument

When erected in 1872, this monument consisted of merely a granite pedestal. The bronze soldier atop was not added until 1908. The *Washington Grays Monument*—honoring a military unit created in Philadelphia in 1822—has been moved several times since it was first installed at Broad Street and Girard Avenue.

Location: In front of the Union League, southwest corner of Broad and Sansom streets.

The *Washington Grays Monument*. *Photo courtesy of Tatiana Heller.*

William McKinley

Less than a year after President William McKinley's untimely death, sculptor Charles Albert Lopez beat out thirty-seven other applicants vying for the McKinley memorial commission. Unfortunately, Lopez himself died before completing his task, and his friend Isidore Konti was selected to finish the project. Assisting Konti with the design was architect Albert R. Ross. At the base of the twenty-two-ton red granite pedestal on which a nine-foot heroic bronze of McKinley is standing are allegorical figures, representing Wisdom as a mature woman and Youth as a young boy. The $30,000 cost for this memorial was borne by private donations.

The McKinley memorial was unveiled on June 6, 1908, following a grand military parade. Afterwards, former United States District Attorney James A. Mack delivered the memorial address at the Academy of Music.

McKinley was born in Niles, Ohio, in 1843. Prior to his election as the twenty-fifth president of the United States, this Union Civil War veteran served for fourteen years in the House of Representatives and two terms as the governor of his home state. Before holding political office, McKinley opened a law firm in Canton, Ohio, and shortly afterwards was a prosecutor for Stark County. During McKinley's first term in the White House, the United States fought a quick war with Spain (1898), resulting in a Spanish defeat, and Spain's loss of Cuba, the Philippines, and Guam. While attending the Pan-American Exposition in Buffalo, New York, in September of 1901, McKinley was fatally shot by crazed anarchist Leon Czolgosz. He died eight days after the attack, becoming the third U.S. president to be assassinated, after Abraham Lincoln and James A. Garfield. For his crime Czolgosz went to the electric chair in New York's Auburn Prison on October 28. Former First Lady Ida McKinley, plagued by ill health since the loss of two daughters in 1873, died six years after her husband.

Location: South side of City Hall, Broad and Market streets.

At the base of the 22-ton red granite pedestal on which a nine-foot heroic bronze of McKinley is standing are allegorical figures, representing Wisdom as a mature woman and Youth as a young boy. *Photo courtesy of Tatiana Heller.*

William Penn (atop City Hall)

The original plans for Philadelphia's City Hall, drawn up by architect John McArthur, Jr., called for the figure of Justice to be placed atop the building. But Justice was supplanted by a huge bronze sculpture of William Penn, cast in 1889 by Tacony Iron and Metal Works. The sculptor was Alexander Milne Calder, who was born in Scotland in 1868 and came to Philadelphia as a young man. His son, Alexander Stirling Calder, would later design the figures for the Swann Memorial Fountain in Logan Square. The elder Calder was also placed in charge of modeling the dozens of smaller sculptures in and on City Hall, like the figures of Swedish settlers and Native Americans at the base of the clock tower's dome.

The enormity of Calder's sculpture can hardly be appreciated from street level, the viewpoint of nearly all visitors to City Hall. The thirty-six-foot, twenty-seven-ton statue of Penn faces northeast, and clutches in its left hand the charter of Pennsylvania, given to Penn in 1682 by King Charles II of England. However, when the finished Penn was exhibited in 1892, prior to its being placed atop the City Hall clock tower, a director of the Pennsylvania Academy of the Fine Arts noticed that the seal on the charter in Penn's hand was that of Queen Victoria, not King Charles II. He successfully argued that because of this historical inaccuracy the sculpture should not be exhibited at the upcoming World's Colombian Exposition in Chicago as planned (Wainwright: 108). *William Penn* was installed atop City Hall without ceremony in 1894.

For many years, no building in the city of Philadelphia was higher than this statue of William Penn. In 1987, the sixty-story One Liberty Place complex at 16th and Market streets, by developer Willard G. Rouse, became the first structure to break this unwritten rule.

Location: Atop City Hall, 15th and Market streets.

The thirty-six-foot, twenty-seven-ton statue of William Penn has been in place atop City Hall since 1894. From the ground he doesn't look quite so big. *Photo courtesy of Tatiana Heller.*

William Penn

In England, William Penn's grandson, John Penn, purchased this six-foot lead statue of his grandfather, and later donated it to the Pennsylvania Hospital. The inscription on the statue's base reads "John Penn A.D. 1804." John Cheere is believed to have sculpted the statue around 1774.

Location: Pennsylvania Hospital, north side of Pine Street between 8th and 9th streets.

William Penn, circa 1774 by John Cheere. *Photo courtesy of Tatiana Heller.*

Charles J. Buckley Memorial

A memorial within a memorial is the large rock bearing the inscription "In Memory of / PFC Charles J. Buckley USMC / 1949-1968 / And of other Americans / who gave their lives in / the Republic of Vietnam." The idea of turning the small parcel of land at the northeast corner of Germantown Avenue and Hartwell Lane into a park had been discussed by area residents for some time. A few months after the death of eighteen-year-old Marine Charles J. Buckley in Vietnam on December 21, 1968, his friends and family renewed the initiative, forming a memorial committee to establish a park in his name. Area shopkeeper Martha Hutchinson began the fund drive by contributing $75 out of what would eventually become a $6,000 project, borne by community donations. Architect Anthony Walmsley, whose wife Helga was the chairwoman of the Chestnut Hill Community Association's (CHCA) Parks Committee, designed the landscaping. The bronze memorial plaque cost about $160.

The park's dedication was held on Saturday, June 2, 1973. Among the 100 or so people in attendance were memorial committee members, local clergy, a Marine honor guard detachment, and Buckley's parents and two younger siblings—his brother Vincent and sister Bonnie. In 1976, the park received a citation from Philadelphia Mayor Frank L. Rizzo, recognizing it as a Bicentennial attraction. Buckley Park underwent renovations in 1992.

Location: Buckley Park, Germantown Avenue and Hartwell Lane, Chestnut Hill.

The memorial to PFC Charles J. Buckley USMC (1949–1968). *Photo courtesy of Ralph J. Rogers.*

Chestnut Hill and Mount Airy World War I Memorial

An elongated, Celtic cross atop a four-tiered pedestal bears the inscription: "In loving memory of the men / of Chestnut Hill and Mt. Airy / Who died in the World War / France, 1918 / They challenge us to hold more precious than mortal life / Ideals of Honour, Justice and Righteousness. / They counted not their lives dear unto themselves."

Location: Germantown Avenue and Mermaid Lane.

Chestnut Hill and Mount Airy World War I Memorial. Photo courtesy of Stan Horwitz.

Henry Melchior Muhlenberg

Henry Melchior Muhlenberg was born in Eimbeck, Prussia, on September 6, 1711. He came to America in 1742, short on funds but endowed with faith and determination. A mistaken belief is that Muhlenberg established the first Lutheran church in America, but a congregation had been meeting at Falkner's Swamp (now Gilbertsville, Pennsylvania) since 1725, and a church was erected in the 1740s. A year after his arrival, Muhlenberg built a modest stone church in Trappe, Montgomery County, Pennsylvania, calling this house of worship Augustus Lutheran Church. There he preached to his flock in both German and English. That same year, Muhlenberg founded a school for boys in Falkner's Swamp.

Augustus Lutheran Church, also known as "the old Trappe Church," was replaced by a new building in the 1850s.

The elder Muhlenberg continued his pastoral duties well into his seventies, when failing health forced him to curtail his activities somewhat. In 1784, Muhlenberg received a doctor of divinity degree from the University of Pennsylvania. After a brief illness, Muhlenberg died in Trappe on October 7, 1787, and was buried in the graveyard of the church that he founded.

This 1917 memorial by J. Otto Schweizer features a bronze likeness of Muhlenberg standing in front of and in between other seated figures on his left and right. The peripheral figures near the center barely emerge from the bronze plate, but the closer the other figures get towards the ends of the memorial, the more depth and dimension they assume. The inscription reads "Patriarch of the Lutheran Church in America / Pastor in Philadelphia / 1742-1787."

 Location: Lutheran Theological Seminary, Germantown Avenue and Allens Lane.

Henry Melchior Muhlenberg, 1917 by J. Otto Schweizer. Photo courtesy of John Kahler.

Chinatown 6

Friendship Gate of Chinatown

The great, glittering gate that for twenty-six years has spanned the intersection of 10th and Cherry streets was initially installed not for purely aesthetic purposes, nor as merely a sparkling salutation from the city's Chinatown section. Both Philadelphia and its sister city of Tianjin, China, sought to foster a mutually beneficial cultural (and economic) exchange. That exchange—as well as plans for the elaborate arch—seemed in doubt when Peking reacted angrily to America's granting asylum to Chinese tennis player Hu Na in April of 1983. Hu had defected nine months earlier when she was with her team at a tournament in California. Philadelphia City Council had already appropriated $197,000—about half the cost—for the Friendship Gate when the Chinese government announced that it was suspending all cultural exchanges with the United States.

In spite of this, the project went ahead as planned, and the dedication was held on January 31, 1984. Twelve visiting artisans, eleven of whom were from Tianjin, had remained in Philadelphia for two months while working on the gate. They in turn were supervised by a team of Chinese engineers. Local laborers handled the actual installation. The Chinese characters on the front read "Philadelphia Chinatown."

The *Friendship Gate* was designed by architect Sabrina Soong, a native of Taiwan who emigrated to the United States in 1965. Soong, who founded her own architectural firm in the city, was actively involved in the revitalization of Chinatown, and a member and past president of the Philadelphia Chinatown Development Corporation. She died of cancer in 2006.

The *Friendship Gate* was designed by architect Sabrina Soong, a native of Taiwan who emigrated to the United States in 1965. *Photo courtesy of Vlad Ringe.*

In 2004, the *Friendship Gate* underwent extensive renovations, as many of the terra cotta tiles were missing, much of the paint had faded, and many of the lights had burned out.

Location: Across 10th Street, north of 10th and Cherry streets, Chinatown.

Abraham Lincoln

Nearly 150 years later, the Civil War remains America's bloodiest conflict, with over 600,000 fatalities. The president who had pledged to heal his sundered nation did not live long enough to fulfill his promise. Less than one week after the Confederate surrender at Appomattox Courthouse, he was assassinated while watching the play *Our American Cousin* at Ford's theater in Washington, D.C. Numerous northern cities sought to memorialize their martyred leader, Philadelphia among them. On September 22, 1871, Philadelphia officially did so with the unveiling of a nine-and-a-half-foot seated bronze statue of the sixteenth president.

Sculptor Randolph Rogers conceived the austere memorial, working from his studio in Rome. The bronze likeness of Lincoln was cast at The Royal Foundry in Munich (in what was then Prussia), while the twenty-two-and-a-half-foot granite base was supplied by Struthers and Son of Philadelphia. Rogers received about $19,000 for the memorial, which features quotes from Lincoln inscribed on the back and sides of the base, and on the front, the words, "To Abraham Lincoln From a Grateful People." The piece remained at East River (now Kelly) and Lemon Hill drives until 2002, before being transported to its current location.

Originally, the design committee of Philadelphia's Lincoln Monument Association wrote to five sculptors, inviting them to submit ideas. Three of the sculptors promptly declined, and a contest soon ensued between Rogers and Thomas Ball, the latter in Florence, Italy. Over the next year-and-a-half, both men corresponded regularly with the Association, sharing their designs, which underwent numerous revisions. The committee even waived its initial stipulation that Lincoln be depicted standing, although both Rogers and Ball had independently conceived of memorials featuring a standing Lincoln beckoning a kneeling slave to rise to freedom. Rogers was finally selected in March of 1868 (Wainwright: 47-49).

Location: Kelly and Sedgely drives.

This memorial to President Abraham Lincoln, by sculptor Randolph Rogers, was unveiled on September 22, 1871. *Photo courtesy of Peter J. Obst.*

Alexander von Humboldt

The theory that mental acuity fosters longevity might be bolstered by the example of Prussian scientist Alexander von Humboldt, who died in his hometown of Berlin five weeks before his ninetieth birthday. After the death of their father, an army officer, Humboldt and his older brother Wilhelm were raised by their mother. Humboldt began his career in 1792 as a government mining supervisor. His official duties, however, proved to be no impediment to his loftier ambitions.

Humboldt's life spanned nearly a century, and his work spanned several scientific disciplines, including geology, botany, meteorology, geomagnetism, and biology. His interest in other cultures was as keen as his interest in science; he was especially fascinated with ancient South American civilizations, which he had occasion to study during a prolonged expedition near the turn of the nineteenth century. Accompanying him on this five-year trek was French botanist Aimé Bonpland. In 1804, as the final leg of his journey, Humboldt visited the United States before returning home in August. His research laid the groundwork for future scientists, among them Charles Darwin. *Kosmos*, Humboldt's comprehensive scientific compendium, was published in five volumes between 1845 and 1862.

The sculpture of the great Prussian scientist, by Frederick Johann Heinrich Drake, was installed in 1871. The inscription reads: "Alexander von Humboldt / Born Sept. 14, 1769 / Died May 6, 1859 / Dedicated to the City of Philadelphia / by its German citizens." The laying of the monument's cornerstone took place following a parade on Monday, September 13, 1869, intended to mark the centenary of Humboldt's birth. The festivities concluded the following day with a concert, and speeches in both German and English. The chairman of the monument committee was William J. Horstmann, who at the time was also president of Philadelphia's German Society.

Location: Martin Luther King Drive and Black Road, Fairmount Park.

Alexander von Humboldt, 1871 by Frederick Johann Heinrich Drake. *Photo courtesy of Stan Horwitz.*

A fifteen-foot marble statue of Moses stands atop a fifteen-foot mound of uneven stones.
Photo courtesy of Peter J. Obst.

Catholic Total Abstinence Union Fountain

A mixed motif characterizes the *Catholic Total Abstinence Union Fountain*, which features a fifteen-foot marble statue of Moses atop a fifteen-foot mound of uneven stones. The Hebrew prophet is at the center of a forty-foot diameter marble basin. This in turn is surrounded by a circular wall bearing medallions featuring Revolutionary War figures—Tadeusz Kosciuszko, Comte de Grasse, Casimir Pulaski, Lafayette, George Gordon Meade (the grandfather of the famous Civil War general), and Penobscot Indian chief Orono. A medallion featuring Colonel Stephen Moylan was planned but never completed; his name appears without an accompanying image. Except for a statue of Father Theobald Matthew, known as the Apostle of Temperance, all of the other statues represent individuals associated with the

Medallions featuring a likeness of Tadeusz Kosciuszko, Casimir Pulaski, and Lafayette. *Photos courtesy of Peter J. Obst.*

Revolutionary War: Commodore John Barry, Archbishop John Carroll and Charles Carroll, a signer of the Declaration of Independence. Each nine-foot statue is mounted upon a pedestal of proportionate height, and each has a drinking fountain. The cost for the monument came to $56,000.

With his left hand, Moses clutches the Ten Commandments and a small staff, while his right hand points towards the sky. Original designs called for the Hebrew prophet to be striking a rock with his staff, causing water to issue forth.

In July of 1910, thirty-four years after the fountain's dedication, the statue of Father Theobald Matthew was badly damaged by a lightning strike. Sculptor Herman Kirn, who at the time was in his sixties and had only one arm, repaired the sculpture almost seamlessly, which included attaching the head to the body with an interior iron rod. The statue was rededicated on Memorial Day the following year.

Born in Germany, Kirn emigrated to the United States when he was six. After completing high school he returned to Europe for several years and received his artistic training. Kirn later lost an arm when a piece of a statue that he was sculpting fell on him. Unable to continue as a sculptor, Kirn was appointed caretaker of the statuary in Fairmount Park, and served in this capacity for thirty years (NewsBank). He died in 1920 at the age of seventy-two.

Location: North Concourse Drive and State Street.

Ellen Phillips Samuel Memorial

The Ploughman, 1938 by J. Wallace Kelly. *Photo courtesy of Peter J. Obst.*

Without the accompanying inscriptions, many of the sculptures dotting this half-mile plot of ground along the Schuylkill River would be inscrutable to visitors. But if they seem like abstract representations, this is precisely what they are meant to be: symbolizing ideals, institutions, and classes of people rather than individual human beings. Even so, they are not totally devoid of pathos; the kneeling, nearly-naked statues of *The Ploughman*, *The Immigrant*, *The Miner*, and *The Slave* exude humility. The ramrod posture of *The Statesman* suggests a slight arrogance, and although the facial features are bland, the figure is reminiscent of George Washington. *The Puritan's* large hands clutch a rifle to his body defiantly.

Like most large-scale monuments, the Ellen Phillips Samuel Memorial was assembled piecemeal over a number of years—in this case, twenty-seven. Samuel, who died in 1913, was a member of the Fairmount Park Art Association, and a bequest in her will called for establishing a memorial representing different periods in the history of America. In soliciting sculptors for this prodigious project, the Association held three international exhibitions, in 1933, 1940, and 1949. The memorial, which was officially completed in 1960, contains sixteen sculptures from fifteen different artists. (Harry Rosin created both *The Puritan* and *The Quaker*).

The Samuel Memorial is divided into three terraces, each with specific themes. The overall chronology follows south to north, commencing with *The Birth of a Nation* and *The Settling of the Seaboard*. These "anchor sculptures" are accompanied by *The Puritan, The Quaker, The Revolutionary Soldier,* and *The Statesman*. The central terrace, which was completed first, contains bronze embodiments of *Spanning the Continent*, referring to the westward expansion across America, and *Welcoming to Freedom*, commemorating the newfound liberty of those formerly in bondage, and those seeking opportunity on the shores of a welcoming nation. Appropriately included are *The Ploughman, The Miner, The Immigrant*, and *The Slave*. Seeming out of place in the center of these limestone sculptures is Jacques Lipchitz's cumbersome bronze *The Spirit of Enterprise*. The study concludes at the north terrace with the granite statues of *The Preacher, The Poet, The Scientist*, and *The Laborer*. *Social Consciousness*, Jacob Epstein's massive bronze, was originally intended for the north terrace as well, but was too big. The piece found a permanent home behind the art museum.

Location: Kelly Drive, south of West Girard Avenue.

Spanning the Continent, 1937 by Robert Laurent. *Photo courtesy of Peter J. Obst.*

The Miner, 1938 by John B. Flannagan. *Photo courtesy of Peter J. Obst.*

The Spirit of Enterprise, 1960 by Jacques Lipchitz. *Photo courtesy of Peter J. Obst.*

The Slave, 1940 by Helene Sardeau. *Photo courtesy of Peter J. Obst.*

Welcoming to Freedom, 1939 by Maurice Sterne. *Photo courtesy of Peter J. Obst.*

The Immigrant, 1940 by Heinz Warneke. *Photo courtesy of Peter J. Obst.*

The Preacher, 1952 by Waldemar Raemisch. *Photo courtesy of Peter J. Obst.*

The Poet, 1954 by Jose de Creeft. *Photo courtesy of Peter J. Obst.*

The Scientist, 1955 by Khoren der Harootian. (See Young Meher). *Photo courtesy of Peter J. Obst.*

The Laborer, 1958 by Ahron Ben-Shmuel. *Photo courtesy of Peter J. Obst.*

The Birth of a Nation, 1943 by Henry Kreis. *Photo courtesy of Peter J. Obst.*

The Revolutionary Soldier, 1943 by Erwin Frey. *Photo courtesy of Peter J. Obst.*

The Quaker, 1942 by Harry Rosin. *Photo courtesy of Peter J. Obst.*

The Puritan, 1943 by Harry Rosin. *Photo courtesy of Peter J. Obst.*

Franz Schubert

During his brief time on earth—he died two months shy of thirty-two—Franz Schubert produced an impressive array of musical material, including *leiden* (German lyrical songs), sonatas, quartets, octets, chamber music, and operas, the latter which met with little success. Schubert held Mozart and Beethoven in the highest esteem; he even met Beethoven on at least two occasions and was a pallbearer at his funeral. Such was his regard for the German writer Goethe that Schubert set no less than thirty of his poems to music. After receiving copies of the young Schubert's efforts, however, Goethe remained unmoved; possibly he considered the initiative presumptuous. Schubert at times approached projects with unbridled enthusiasm, only to inexplicably abandon them. This was particularly true of his symphonies, all but one (Symphony No. 9 in C Major) of which were left unfinished at the time of his death.

Schubert taught periodically at his father's Vienna school, but never with any enthusiasm. He frequently took up lodgings with male friends and acquaintances, such as the law student Franz von Schober, the artist Moritz von Schwind, and the opera singer Johann Vogl, with whom he went on extended trips into the countryside. Some details of these relationships suggest that Schubert may have been homosexual.

The last six years of Schubert's life were both productive and painful, marked by renewed operatic efforts, the completion of his aforementioned Symphony No. 9, several piano sonatas, a concert performance, and recurring bouts of venereal disease. The talented Austrian composer and musician succumbed to complications from syphilis on November 19, 1828.

Location: Horticultural Center, Belmont Avenue and Montgomery Drive.

Franz Schubert, 1891 by Henry Baerer.

Frederick Graff Memorial

Although long since replaced by modern treatment plants, Philadelphia's Water Works has remained a source of awe and inspiration, as much for its artistry as for its ingenuity. Completed in 1822, the Water Works utilized an efficient system of hydraulics designed by engineer Frederick Graff (1774–1847) to extract water from the Schuylkill River for use by city residents. The impetus for the project was the need for safe, clean drinking water: Philadelphia had already experienced several outbreaks of water-borne illnesses. The Water Works remained functional for nearly eighty years, periodically undergoing technological updates to ensure peak efficiency. Today, its pediments, porticos, and columns in descending symmetry stare silently across the river. The quaint stone buildings form a line of ancient architecture that seems to float on the waters of yesteryear.

Graff served as chief engineer of the Water Works until his death in 1847, at which point his son, Frederick, Jr., was appointed. This marble and granite memorial was installed the following year.

Location: Fairmount Water Works Interpretive Center, 640 Waterworks Drive.

The Frederick Graff Memorial. Photo courtesy of Tatiana Heller.

General Ulysses S. Grant

The eminent Daniel Chester French collaborated with his former student Edward C. Potter on this equestrian statue of the Union's most renowned general, Ulysses S. Grant (1822–1885). French designed Grant and Potter designed Grant's horse. A seven-member Grant Memorial Committee was formed in July 1885, a committee that eventually selected French from an initial list of seven possible artists. The bronze memorial is fourteen-and-a-half feet in height, larger than the one-and-a-half times life-sized originally proposed. The unveiling was held on April 27, 1899, which would have been Grant's seventy-seventh birthday.

Grant's critics saw him as a butcher or a drunk, but his strongest advocate was President Lincoln himself, who, upon being told that his favorite general imbibed too much, supposedly replied, "Tell me what he's drinking, so I can buy a case for all of my generals." While the story is of dubious authenticity, it nevertheless illustrates the confidence that the president had in Grant. In March of 1864, Lincoln appointed Grant commander of all Union forces. Grant's tactical skills and morale were impressive: on several occasions he rallied his harried Federal troops and turned the tide of losing battles. His casualties were also staggering, and prior to his accepting the Confederate surrender at Appomattox in April of 1865, Grant's army took several thrashings from Robert E. Lee (Wooster: 9).

Grant's military glory proved an effective political stepping stone, and he was twice elected president, in 1868 and 1876. But his political savvy fell far short of his military puissance, and his administration was tainted by scandal. He likewise had failed as a businessman, both early in his adult life and following his presidency. Writing his memoirs proved a more successful endeavor, earning his family nearly half a million dollars. Grant, however, did not live to see the fruits of these last labors, succumbing to throat cancer shortly after completing the task (Ibid.).

Location: Kelly and Fountain Green drives.

The eminent Daniel Chester French collaborated with his former student Edward C. Potter on this equestrian statue of the Union's most renowned general, Ulysses S. Grant (1822–1885). *Photo courtesy of Peter J. Obst.*

George and Meta Conor-Wood Memorial

This simple, symmetrical memorial to George and Meta Conor-Wood is basically a carved tablet on a retaining wall. Depicted is a seated Indian brave dressed in a loincloth, a single feather protruding from his headband. His arms are outstretched, as if he is reaching for the four does flanking him on either side. On the outer edges of the rectangular stone tablet are the outlines of trees.

Meta Josephine Conor-Wood died in 1908, thirteen years after her husband George, with whom she shared twenty-two years of marriage. On March 29, 1909, the city of Philadelphia accepted a bequest from the late Mrs. Conor-Wood for artwork—paintings and statuary—to be known as the George and Meta Conor-Wood Collection, and kept in Memorial Hall or the Art Gallery. Two years later, the city reversed course, rejecting the bequest on the determination that the artwork was of inferior quality, and estimating that acquiring it would cost the city $20,000. The sixty-two members of the Common Council voted unanimously to reject the collection. But the dubious bequest was to resurface, at least in part: on January 27, 1918, a notice appeared in the *New York Evening Post* for a sale of oil paintings from the Conor-Wood estate, to be held in Madison Square.

The artist for the *Conor-Wood Memorial*, Ahron Ben-Shmuel, began carving various shapes and objects when he was a young boy, graduating to progressively harder materials. Later, he apprenticed for three years with a monument carver. He liked working with "difficult"

George and Meta Conor-Wood Memorial. Photo courtesy of Stan Horwitz.

media, such as marble and granite, examples of which includes his busts *Father* (1923) and *Head of a Young Poet* (1929), *Boxers* (1937), and the figure of *The Laborer* (1949) for the Ellen Philips Samuel Memorial (James A. Michener Museum). Ben-Shmuel received a Guggenheim Fellowship in 1937. The New York native spent nearly the last two decades of his life in Jerusalem, where he died in 1984.

Location: Martin Luther King Drive and Black Road.

Giuseppe Verdi

Giuseppe Verdi (1813-1901) was the most acclaimed opera composer of his time—arguably of all time. He produced more than two-thirds of his creative output in the first two decades of his career—twenty works in about as many years, with a lifetime total of twenty-seven. His most powerful pieces combined lofty subjects with plots bordering on the melodramatic, yet skillfully blended with political intrigue. That Verdi remained popular in a highly-fickle business was a testament to his talent and appeal. Among his best-known operas are *Rigoletto, La Traviata, Don Carlos, Attila,* and *Il Trovatore.*

Verdi's enthusiasm slowed down after his initial prolific period, and he became jaded and morose, even referring to the opera as "a sewer." Some of his sentiments likely stemmed from the death of his first wife, Margherita, and both his children, early in his career, although he found companionship in a soprano named Giuseppina Strepponi, whom Verdi married after years of cohabitation. He purchased a large estate, and would have been content to spend the rest of his days farming, but was drawn out of his self-imposed exile by several more commissions. Always a fan of the Bard, Verdi wrote the Shakespearean operas *Macbeth, Othello,* and *Falstaff,* which was to be his last. As a final act of philanthropy, Verdi founded a home for retired composers and musicians.

Location: The Horticultural Center, Belmont Avenue and Montgomery Drive.

A bust of Giuseppe Verdi sits atop its pedestal in the park, surrounded by verdant spring foliage. One source says Ettore Ferrari was the sculptor, another source says G. B. Bashanellifusi.

Henry Howard Houston

This 1900 sculpture was by John Massey Rhind. Houston (1820–1895) was a railroad tycoon who owned a great deal of real estate in the Chestnut Hill section of the city. Rhind received $11,000 for the piece.

Location: Lincoln Drive and Harvey Street.

Henry Howard Houston, 1900 by John Massey Rhind. *Photo courtesy of Stan Horwitz.*

James A. Garfield

Some viewers may remark upon the disproportionate size of the "secondary" figure in Augustus Saint-Gaudens' 1895 monument to assassinated President James A. Garfield—the allegorical representation of the Republic—to the "primary" one, the heroic bust of Garfield. More than twice the height of the bronze bust above her, Republic stands behind an unusually large shield whose inscription reads: "JAMES ABRAM / GARFIELD / PRESIDENT OF THE / UNITED STATES / MDCCC- / LXXXI." Her right hand holds a partially-drawn sword. Architect Stanford White assisted the sculptor with the design and eventually with the landscaping. The unveiling came in 1896, seven years after Saint-Gaudens signed the original contract and fifteen years after Garfield's untimely death at the hands of a disgruntled office seeker, Charles J. Guiteau.

Saint-Gaudens was a highly respected sculptor, but his dilatory manner often put him at odds with his employers. In 1893, the artist decided that he wanted to revise his original plans for the Garfield monument, and asked the Fairmount Park Art Association for a new contract. In a letter to the Association, John T. Morris, one of the five committee members overseeing the monument, complained bitterly about Saint-Gaudens, writing that the sculptor was "treating us miserably." But the new contract was granted, and Saint-Gaudens' fee for the amended project rose from $15,000 to $20,000 (Wainwright: 181).

Garfield was born in Cuyahoga County, Ohio, in 1831. Prior to his eighteen-year stint as a congressman for his state, he was a professor and president of Western Reserve Eclectic Institute in Hiram, Ohio. Fighting for the Union during the Civil War, Garfield attained the rank of major general. In 1880, he defeated fellow Civil War general Winfield Scott Hancock, a Democrat, to become the twentieth president of the United States. Shot in the back at a train station in July of 1881, Garfield succumbed to his injuries on September 19, two months shy of his fiftieth birthday. He was laid to rest in Lakeview Cemetery in Cleveland, Ohio. The assassin, Guiteau, was hanged the following June.

Location: Kelly Drive and Girard Avenue Bridge.

More than twice the height of the bronze bust above her, Republic stands behind an unusually large shield. *Photo courtesy of Peter J. Obst.*

Johann Christoph Friedrich von Schiller

This memorial to German poet and playwright Johann Christoph Friedrich von Schiller (1759–1805) was commissioned by Canstatter Volkfest Verein, a German-American fraternal organization. The laying of the cornerstone, which preceded the actual dedication by nearly a year, was perhaps as impressive, and arguably made the October 25, 1886, unveiling extraneous. A number of attendees—German dignitaries residing in the city, and freemasons—chartered a train from Broad and Callowhill streets to Centennial Station, in proximity to Horticultural Hall. A special silver, gold-plated trowel with a diamond-encrusted handle was used for the Masonic ceremony, after which a chorus from the United German singers performed, followed by an orchestral rendition of *True German Heart* (NewsBank).

Location: The Horticultural Center, Belmont Avenue and Montgomery Drive.

Johann Christoph Friedrich von Schiller, 1886 by Heinrich Carl Johan Manger.

Johann Wolfgang von Goethe

This statue of Goethe was commissioned by the same German-American organization that in 1885 commissioned a monument to Johann Christoph Friedrich von Schiller, and was meant as a companion piece. The foundation stone was laid during a November 14, 1887, ceremony, and drew a sizeable crowd. Sculptor Heinrich Carl Johan Manger (simply known as Henry Manger), working out of his studio in Roxborough, completed a model for the nine-foot bronze in May of 1889, and by December of that year, the statue and pedestal were cast by Bureau Brothers foundry in Philadelphia. The dedication was held on May 30, 1891. The $12,000 cost of the statue was raised by the Goethe Monument Association.

Goethe (1749–1832) was the son of a wealthy lawyer, who expected his son to follow in his footsteps. The young Goethe obligingly studied law at Leipzig, then at Strasbourg, but decided that he was better-suited for literary rather than legal endeavors. He became good friends with Schiller, someone with whom he could share camaraderie as well as his passion for writing, and Goethe was devastated by Schiller's death in 1805. Although Goethe's output was phenomenal, he is best known for *Die Lieden Des Jungen Werther* (*The Sorrows of Young Werther*, 1774) and *Faust* (written in two parts, 1808 and 1832).

 Location: The Horticultural Center, Belmont Avenue and Montgomery Drive.

Johann Wolfgang von Goethe, 1890 by Heinrich Carl Johan Manger. Inscriptions on the pedestal read, in both English and German, "Dedicated by the German-American citizens of Philadelphia." *Photo courtesy of Tatiana Heller*.

John B. Kelly

John B. Kelly (1889-1960) was one of ten children born in Philadelphia to Irish immigrants. In the sport of sculling, in which each rower uses a pair of oars, the young Kelly excelled, garnering 126 straight victories in his first year of competing in races on the Schuylkill River. In 1920, Kelly applied to England's Henley Royal Regatta, but was turned down because as a bricklayer, he was not a "gentleman." But Kelly would have his revenge: not only did he defeat the Henley champion, Jack Beresford, in that year's Olympics in Antwerp, Belgium, but his son, John B. Kelly II, won the Henley in 1947 and 1949. Based on a photograph, Harry Rosin's sculpture depicts Kelly competing at the 1920 Olympics (FPAA).

On the evening of September 22, 1920, a banquet was held in Philadelphia in honor of "Jack" Kelly, who won the single sculls event at the Olympics, and in honor of Kelly's cousin, Paul V. Costello, who with Kelly took the doubles championship. The pair repeated this feat at the Paris Olympics four years later.

Although known primarily as a rower, Kelly was a versatile athlete who participated in numerous sports. A formidable boxer, he won a dozen heavyweight boxing matches while in the military during the First World War. The business world was kind to Kelly, as well; he and two of his brothers operated a lucrative construction firm, and perhaps Kelly's financial success emboldened him to try his hand at politics. He was Philadelphia's Democratic Party Chairman from 1934 to 1941, during which time he waged an unsuccessful mayoral campaign against Republican Samuel D. Wilson. His aspirations for a United States Senate seat in 1936 likewise foundered. Kelly and his wife had four children, among them actress Grace Kelly (1928–1982). He died in Philadelphia at the age of seventy.

Location: River side of Kelly Drive, at the north end of the reviewing stands.

John B. Kelly (1889–1960): athlete, politician, businessman, Philadelphia legend. *Photo courtesy of Peter J. Obst.*

Law, Prosperity, and Power

Moved to its present site in 1938, this marble statuary group was originally created for the post office and federal building at 9th and Chestnut streets. The structure at the previous location was demolished the year prior. Despite the name, Daniel Chester French's 1880 sculpture depicts, from left to right, the representations of Power, Law and Prosperity, respectively.

Perhaps the best-known American sculptor of the nineteenth and early twentieth centuries—with the possible exception of Augustus Saint-Gaudens—Daniel Chester French was born in Exeter, New Hampshire, in 1850. He possessed both considerable talent and drive, the latter with which he was able to learn his vocation without much formal training. Still, trips to Italy and France helped hone his sculptural skills. The young artist's debut, so to speak, came in 1874 with his *Minute Man* for the town of Concord, Massachusetts. This bronze work was commissioned to commemorate the 100th anniversary of the Battle of Lexington and Concord, where "the shot heard 'round the world" was fired. During his career, French executed a number of public and private memorials, several funerary sculptures comprising the latter. French is best known for his immense, seated marble statue of slain President Abraham Lincoln, completed in 1920 for the Lincoln Memorial. Some of his other famous pieces include a seated bronze of John Harvard at the university bearing his name (1884), the Thomas Gallaudet statue in Washington, D.C. (1888), the bronze doors for the Boston Public Library (1904), and the Samuel F. DuPont Fountain, also in Washington, D.C. (1917). French died in 1931 at the age of 81. Chesterwood, his home and studio in Stockbridge, Massachusetts, is now a museum.

Location: South George's Hill Drive, Mann Music Center.

Law, Prosperity, and Power, by Daniel Chester French. *Photo courtesy of Stan Horwitz.*

Major General George Gordon Meade

The life of Major General George Gordon Meade, to paraphrase Shakespeare's *Twelfth Night*, was an example of both achieving greatness and having greatness thrust upon him. The former he demonstrated by his bravery and leadership both in the Mexican War (1846–1848) and numerous Civil War battles later in his military career. He showed the latter by halting the advance of Robert E. Lee's Army of Northern Virginia at the battle of Gettysburg on July 1-3, 1863. This occurred just days after Meade was appointed head of the Army of the Potomac, a promotion which he accepted unenthusiastically. Although Meade successfully repulsed the Confederate invasion of Northern territory, he was faulted for not pursuing the retreating Southern forces. Afterwards Meade tendered his resignation, which President Lincoln did not accept (Magner: 30).

In 1835, Meade graduated nineteenth out of a class of fifty-three from West Point. After a brief enlistment he took a six-year hiatus from the military, during which he married and did surveying and construction work. Born in Cadiz, Spain, on December 31, 1815, Meade spent most of his boyhood, and much of his adulthood, in Philadelphia, and passed his last few years there, where he served as a Fairmount Park commissioner. Following his death from pneumonia on November 7, 1872, he was interred in the city's famous Laurel Hill Cemetery. His funeral drew thousands of mourners. Within days, Philadelphians assembled a memorial committee to erect a statue to the hero of Gettysburg. But not until 1884 did Alexander Milne Calder receive the $25,000 commission, which he completed for an October 18, 1887, unveiling.

Major General George Gordon Meade, the hero of Gettysburg. *Photo courtesy of Stan Horwitz.*

Calder's bronze equestrian sculpture depicts the general upon his trusty horse, Baldy. The figures of Meade and his mount were cast by the Henry Bonnard Company of New York.

Location: North side of Memorial Hall, North Concourse Drive.

Morton McMichael

Sculpted in 1881 by John H. Mahoney, and installed on October 23, 1882, this memorial is dedicated to former Philadelphia mayor Morton McMichael, a Republican, who held office from 1866 to 1869. McMichael also served as the first president of the Fairmount Park Commission from 1867 until his death in 1879.

This memorial was funded by public donations.

Location: Lemon Hill Drive near Poplar Street.

Philadelphia mayor Morton McMichael, a Republican, who held office from 1866 to 1869. *Photo courtesy of Stan Horwitz.*

Negro Leagues Memorial

Long before Jackie Robinson's 1947 major league debut with the Brooklyn Dodgers, there were many black ballplayers who were as good, and often better, than their white counterparts. But racial segregation trickled down to every strata of society, and professional sports were no exception. Undaunted, in 1920 eight all-black baseball teams formed the National Negro Leagues. This was the start of an athletic adventure that would span more than four decades, and catapult to fame dozens of players who might have otherwise languished in anonymity all of their lives.

Philadelphia was represented in the Negro Leagues by the Stars, who played twenty seasons. The memorial honoring these pioneering black athletes was originally unveiled at the now-defunct Veterans Stadium, where it remained for one month. The piece was then relocated to its permanent home at Belmont and Parkside avenues, the site of the Stars' former ballpark. Among those attending the June 18, 2003, dedication were Mayor John Street, Philadelphia Phillies' shortstop Jimmy Rollins, and five surviving members of the Stars: Bill Cash, Mahlon Duckett, Stanley Glenn, Harold Gould, and Wilmer Harris. (Harris died in 2004.)

Philadelphia sculptor Phil Sumpter has created numerous monuments of prominent black athletes and artists. His commissions include a statue of Pittsburgh Pirates' right fielder Roberto Clemente, and of performer and activist Paul Robeson. Sumpter also designed a statue of Negro Leagues player and Baseball Hall of Fame inductee Julius "Judy" Johnson for the Daniel S. Frawley Stadium in Wilmington, Delaware. In the early 1990s, Sumpter collaborated with artist Cal Massey on the *Patriots of African Descent Monument* in Valley Forge National Historical Park, which honors black Revolutionary War soldiers. Several years ago Sumpter and his wife moved to Puerto Rico.

Location: Southwest corner of Belmont and Parkside avenues.

Negro Leagues Memorial, 2003 by Phil Sumpter. *Photo courtesy of Stan Horwitz.*

Reverend John Witherspoon

The Scottish-born Presbyterian minister Reverend John Witherspoon (1723–1794) was one of the fifty-six signers of the Declaration of Independence, but he is also known for his contributions to the College of New Jersey, later to become Princeton University. He accepted the presidency of the college in 1768, and held the post until his death. During the Revolution, Witherspoon divided his time between his administrative and patriotic duties. The war took a toll on the college, as well as on Witherspoon's health; he was blind towards the end of his life. Fellow Scotsman and signer of the Declaration of Independence, Dr. Benjamin Rush, was instrumental in convincing Witherspoon to accept the position as college president.

Philadelphia's Witherspoon monument was designed by Joseph A. Bailly. An inscription on the side of the pedestal also appears on the pedestal of Thomas Ball's 1909 sculpture of Witherspoon, in Dupont Circle in Washington, D.C.:

> *For my own part, of property I have some, of reputation more. That reputation is staked,*
> *that property is pledged on the issue of this contest: and although these gray hairs must soon*
> *descend into the sepulcher, I would immediately rather that they descend thither by the hand*
> *of the executioner than desert at this crisis the sacred cause of my country.*

Location: Horticultural Center, Belmont Avenue and Montgomery Drive.

Reverend John Witherspoon, circa 1876 by Joseph A. Bailly. *Photo courtesy of Stan Horwitz.*

Schuylkill Navy War Memorial

The Schuylkill Navy of Philadelphia is an organization of amateur rowing clubs established in October of 1858. The original nine "barge clubs" were America, Camilla, Chebucto, Falcon, Independent, Keystone, Neptune, Pennsylvania, and University. The bylaws stated that the Schuylkill Navy was to be headed by a board of five officers—Commodore, Vice-Commodore, Secretary, Treasurer, and Log-Keeper—each to be appointed for a term of one year. The first Commodore of the Schuylkill Navy was Charles M. Prevost.

A plaque featuring the logo of the Schuylkill Navy, this memorial was dedicated on July 4, 1950.

Location: Wall, reviewing stands, river side of Kelly Drive.

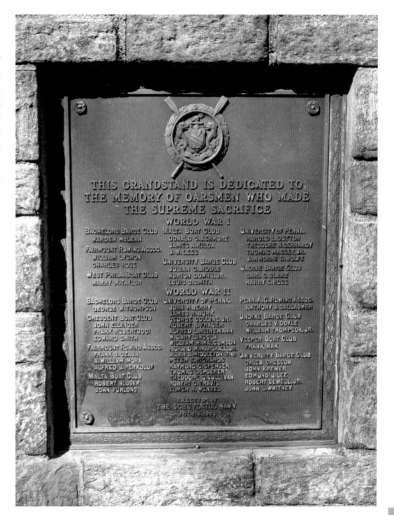

A plaque featuring the logo of the Schuylkill Navy, was dedicated on July 4, 1950.
Photo courtesy of Peter J. Obst.

The *Smith Memorial Arch* took about fifteen years to complete. *Photo courtesy of Peter J. Obst.*

Smith Civil War Memorial
(aka Smith Memorial Arch)

Of the thirteen individuals depicted on the *Smith Civil War Memorial* in West Fairmount Park, three of them have no direct connection to the conflict. Foremost among this trio is wealthy Philadelphian Richard Smith (1821–1894), whose half-a-million dollar bequest financed the grandiose monument. Posing on a stone abutment on the lower right side of the entrance, the fourteen-foot statue of Smith (by Herbert Adams) arguably commands more attention than those of generals George Gordon Meade (by Daniel

Chester French) and John Fulton Reynolds (by Charles Grafly), loftily perched atop a pair of 107-foot Doric columns. Yet Smith's expression is ironically humble, his eyes cast downward. Busts of James H. Windrim (by Samuel Murray), the architect, and John B. Gest (also by Charles Grafly), the executor of Smith's will, occupy alcoves within the semi-circular walls. With the exception of Andrew G. Curtin (by Sir Moses Jacob Ezekiel), Pennsylvania's governor during the Civil War, all of the remaining sculptures are of military commanders from both the army and navy. Flanking the entrance are equestrian statues of generals George B. McClellan (by Bessie O. Potter Vonnoh) and Winfield Scott Hancock (by John Quincy Adams Ward). A pair of eagles (by John Massey Rhind) perches on rounded pedestals at the base of the structure on either side. The granite for this memorial was quarried in Maine.

When plans for the new "*Smith Memorial Arch*" were made public in 1898, Windrim indicated that the designers did not want to emulate the Arc de Triomphe in Paris, lest they be accused of "copying after foreign designs and being deficient in native originality." Although generally optimistic, Windrim cited difficulties in the excavation due to the foundational remnants of the previous structure, demolished in 1874. He gave a tentative date of September 1, 1900, for the completion of the main structure (Newsbank).

The Fairmount Park Art Association was tasked with selecting sculptors for the statues, which they did fairly quickly. But bureaucratic hassles, bickering between the Association members and artists, inaccurate time and cost estimates, and the rescinding and reassigning of contracts significantly prolonged completion of the project (Wainwright: 171-178). The last statue was finally hoisted into place in 1912, fifteen years after the commission first met to discuss the planned memorial.

Location: North Concourse Drive, west of North 41st Street, West Fairmount Park.

Andrew G. Curtin, Pennsylvania's governor during the Civil War, by Sir Moses Jacob Ezekiel. *Photo courtesy of Peter J. Obst.*

Philadelphian Richard Smith (1821–1894), whose half-a-million dollar bequest financed the grandiose monument. *Photo courtesy of Peter J. Obst.*

One of two eagles designed by John Massey Rhind. *Photo courtesy of Peter J. Obst.*

General George B. McClellan, by Bessie O. Potter Vonnoh. *Photo courtesy of Peter J. Obst.*

The Journeyer

Dedicated in June of 1975, this twelve-foot bronze commemorates the nation's bicentennial, which of course occurred thirteen months later. The sculptor was Lindsay Daen, who was born in New Zealand in 1929. Daen received the commission for *The Journeyer* in 1973. He created public monuments in Australia, where he grew up, as well as in Puerto Rico, where he met his second wife and maintained a studio for twenty-two years. *The Journeyer*'s elongated appearance, especially the legs, is characteristic of much of Daen's work (Beale, ed.), with a few notable exceptions.

Location: Belmont Mansion and North Horticultural drives.

The Journeyer, 1975 by Lindsay Daen. *Photo courtesy of Stan Horwitz.*

Thorfinn Karlsefni

Shortly after the death of his wife, Ellen, Bunford Samuel was anxious to implement the provisions in her will establishing sculptures illustrating the history and colonization of North America. First to appear was the statue of Icelandic explorer Thorfinn Karlsefni, unveiled November 20, 1920, on the south terrace of what was to become the Ellen Phillips Samuel Memorial. Also known as *The Viking*, this impressive and intimidating likeness was completed by Einar Jonsson of Reykjavik, Iceland, in 1918, while the artist was in Philadelphia.

Jonsson's Karlsefni leans confidently on a huge battle axe, while a backup weapon, a sheathed broadsword, hangs at his side. Inscribed on his spiked shield in Icelandic are the words: "From the island of the north of ice and fire of blossoming valleys and blue mountains, of the waiting sun and the dreamy mists, the home of the goddess of the Northern Lights" (FPAA). The heroic bronze is about seven feet tall, and stands atop a five-and-a-half-foot granite base. A plaque dated October 9, 1976, provides brief biographical information about Karlsefni: he and 200 followers established a short-lived colony in North America in the early eleventh century, following Leif Ericson's discovery of the continent, and that during this time Karlsefni's son, Snorri, was born.

Trained at Copenhagen's Royal Danish Academy of Fine Arts, Einar Jonsson was the perfect choice to sculpt the figure of Thorfinn Karlsefni. Hailed as Iceland's first sculptor, he often chose themes drawn from historical, mythological, and religious sources. His first public sculpture was *Outlaws*, completed in 1901. In addition to many public monuments, Jonsson executed a number of private commissions, as well. The Einar Jonsson museum in Reykjavik, which opened in 1923, features hundreds of the artist's works, as well as the house in which he and his wife, Anna, lived.

Location: Kelly Drive and Boathouse Row.

Thorfinn Karlsefni, looking formidable in bronze. *Photo courtesy of Peter J. Obst.*

Tuning Fork
(Laurence Katz Memorial)

    An inscription reads: In fond remembrance of / LAWRENCE KATZ / from his friends of / MANN MUSIC CENTER / 1984. The artist was Raymond Granville Barger.

Location: Mann Music Center, North Concourse Drive.

Tuning Fork (Laurence Katz Memorial), 1984 by Raymond Granville Barger. *Photo courtesy of Stan Horwitz.*

Battle of Germantown Memorial

The Battle of Germantown Memorial, dedicated in 1905. *Photo courtesy of Stan Horwitz.*

A ponderous granite stele in Vernon Park bears an inscription reading: "Erected by the Commonwealth of Pennsylvania in commemoration of the Battle of Germantown fought October 4 1777." Etched into the plaque is a map of the battlefield. In February 1903, State Senator John T. Harrison of Philadelphia sponsored a bill appropriating $10,000 for a monument to the historic Revolutionary War battle. Shortly after the monument's installation, controversy erupted over its aesthetic quality. The Germantown Business Men's Association called the memorial "a monstrosity," and added that it should be "hidden away in a cemetery," while the five-member monument committee countered that the critics had no taste in art. Ironically, Senator Harrison never saw the memorial—he died in December of 1903, more than two years before the dedication.

In October of 1777, Germantown was occupied by British and Hessian forces, and General George Washington hatched a plan to retake the town. Germantown—which at that time was not part of Philadelphia—was of strategic significance due to its proximity to the city. Philadelphia was also occupied by forces under British General Sir William Howe. For his basic strategy, Washington envisioned a two-pronged attack led by Brigadier General John Sullivan and General Nathanael Greene. While the initial onslaught against enemy positions looked promising, a number of English troops were holed up in a formidable stone mansion known as Cliveden, owned by Benjamin Chew, a loyalist. American troops wasted considerable time, effort, and ammunition trying to oust their English adversaries, an attempt that proved unsuccessful. Further misfortune befell the invaders elsewhere in the field, when two bodies of American forces mistakenly fired on each other, confused by the heavy smoke and early morning fog. However, although Washington's offensive failed, the battle earned the Colonial army a measure of respect (Ketchum: 214-216).

Location: Vernon Park, Germantown and Chelten avenues.

Civil War Soldiers and Sailors Monument

This monument was dedicated July 4, 1883, to honor Germantown's Civil War dead. The sculptor was John Lacmer, and the pedestal was designed by architect John T. Windrim. The nine-and-a-half-foot statue of the soldier and the thirty-five-foot pedestal are made of granite.

Location: Market Square, Germantown Avenue, and Church Lane (and a replica at Belmont Avenue and South George's Hill Drive).

One of two *Civil War Soldiers and Sailors Monuments*. This image is from the replica at Belmont Avenue and South George's Hill Drive. *Photo courtesy of Tatiana Heller.*

Franz Daniel Pastorius

This mighty marble and granite monument, sculpted by Albert Jaegers in 1917, reveals a seated, bare-chested woman atop a pedestal carved with bas-reliefs on all four sides. Representing the embodiment of civilization, the lady cups a lamp in her right hand. Inscribed on the front of the base are the names of Franz Daniel Pastorius and the twelve German Mennonite settlers who arrived in America on October 6, 1683. The anniversary of their landing was celebrated as German Day.

Exactly when the drive to erect a memorial to the founder of Germantown began is unclear. A *Philadelphia Inquirer* article published on September 23, 1908, reported that a bronze tablet was to be completed by sculptor J. Otto Schweizer on October 6 of that year, and set as the cornerstone of the planned memorial, while a November 11, 1920, story from the same newspaper stated that the initiative did not begin until 1911.

The dedication was held on November 10, 1920, with Philadelphia Mayor J. Hampton Moore accepting the *Pastorius Monument* on behalf of the city. Unveiling the structure was Mary Clossen, whose ancestor Abraham Op Den Graeff was one of the original thirteen settlers. Also present at the ceremony was a descendant of Pastorius himself, Samuel N. Pastorius, who introduced Mayor Moore. The mayor referred to Jaegers' sculpture as "another and worthy memorial of the historic events about Philadelphia, the study and appreciation of which intensify our pride in the foundations upon which our country has grown" (Newsbank). The roughly $50,000 cost for the *Pastorius Monument* was borne half by Congress and half by private subscriptions, mainly the German-American Alliance.

Not everyone was as enthusiastic as Moore about the city's newest sculptural addition. Both during and after the First World War, many residents of Philadelphia were opposed to a monument honoring a German. This anti-German sentiment delayed the completion of

Franz Daniel Pastorius, 1917 by Albert Jaegers. Photo courtesy of Stan Horwitz.

the memorial. Similar resentments during World War II caused the Pastorius monument to be temporarily removed (Wainwright: 279).

Location: Vernon Park, Germantown and Chelten avenues.

Saint Vincent de Paul

A tireless advocate for the poor, sick, and displaced, French priest Vincent de Paul (1580–1660) spent most of his life attempting to alleviate their suffering. Born in the province of Gascony, he left this world with few possessions, much humility, and a legacy that his modesty would have him deny. A traveling priest in his younger days, he had his career and concurrent theological studies interrupted for two years when he was kidnapped by Barbary pirates and held as a slave. He eventually escaped, but his ordeal forever affected him, inspiring his future charity towards those in similar situations. De Paul founded beneficent organizations: the Sisters of Charity and the Daughters of Charity, who helped him minister to the homeless and hungry; the Congregation of Priests of the Mission, comprised of itinerant preachers; the Hospice of the Name of Jesus, for aged infirm men and women; and most notably, a shelter at St. Lazare. This shelter severely taxed the resources available to de Paul and his staff, who were usually short on food, firewood, and space. De Paul also established missions for prisoners and galley slaves, and even managed to send envoys to the Barbary Coast to comfort and, in some cases, purchase the freedom of captured slaves. His humanitarian efforts were frequently hampered by war and pestilence, but he persevered. He was canonized in 1737.

Location: Saint Vincent de Paul Church, East Price and Lena streets.

Saint Vincent de Paul. Photo courtesy of Mary Kay.

Independence Mall 9

Commodore John Barry

Commodore John Barry (1745–1803), the "Father of the American Navy." *Photo courtesy of Peter J. Obst.*

Immortalized in bronze by Philadelphia sculptor Samuel Murray, the Irish-born Commodore John Barry (1745–1803), the "Father of the American Navy," stands in full naval regalia atop an eleven-and-a-half-foot granite pedestal that bears his surname in capital letters. His right hand points at something or someone in the distance, perhaps an approaching British ship. In his left hand is a spyglass. The statue of Barry was presented to the city of Philadelphia on Saturday, March 16, 1907, by the Society of the Friendly Sons of Saint Patrick, of which Samuel Murray was a member, as was Barry. Among those present at the ceremony were the president of the sponsoring organization, General Thomas J. Stewart, Philadelphia Mayor John Weaver, Admiral George W. Melville, who gave the keynote speech, and Barry's great-great-great niece, twelve-year-old Elise Hazel Hepburn, who was given the honor of unveiling the statue. In accepting the statue for the city, Mayor Weaver praised Barry's formidable fighting skills, in particular the commodore's capture of numerous British vessels during the American Revolution.

Emigrating to Philadelphia at a young age, Barry became a merchant mariner prior to his captain's commission in the Continental Navy in 1776. In the latter capacity he commanded four ships throughout the course of the Revolutionary War. Among his greatest victories was the capture of two British ships in 1781, despite being seriously wounded in the battle, and his defeat of the enemy vessel *Sybil* in 1783, while he was captain of the *Alliance*. The only significant blemish on his distinguished naval career occurred in 1778 when his *Raleigh* fell into enemy hands. Barry died at his home in Philadelphia at the age of fifty-eight, and was buried at Old Saint Mary's Cemetery.

Location: 500 Walnut Street, Independence Square.

Jonathan Netanyahu Memorial

The memorial to Jonathan Netanyahu, by Israeli artist Buky S. Schwartz. *Photo courtesy of Stan Horwitz.*

Nineteenth century sculptors would likely have dismissed abstract memorials as too vague, or lacking any discernible meaning entirely. Even the aforementioned *Galusha Pennypacker Memorial* in Logan Square, while not a direct representation of the subject, nevertheless contains somewhat recognizable symbols. But modern artists and audiences alike understand what their forbears may have failed to grasp: that abstraction can often capture a poignancy that traditional sculptures cannot. The Vermont marble monolith torn asunder into four separate slabs, their pinkish insides facing outwards, actually evinces the sensation of an injured object. The representation is meant to be of a life cut short, in this case, the life of Lieutenant Colonel Jonathan "Yoni" Netanyahu. The inscription reads: "Entebbe, Jonathan Netanyahu, July 4, 1976. They were swifter than eagles, they were stronger than lions, the bow of Jonathan bowed not back." The quote is adapted from II Samuel 1:22-23.

Netanyahu led a 1976 Israeli commando raid to free 104 Jewish hostages whose Air France flight was hijacked and forced to land in Entebbe, Uganda. The hijackers, who sought the release of fifty-three terrorists, were given safe haven by Ugandan dictator Idi Amin. A week after their capture, on July 4, the hostages were rescued in an almost flawless military strike by Netanyahu and his men. All eight hijackers were killed, as well as forty to fifty Ugandan soldiers. Three hostages also died, however, and about ten were wounded. Netanyahu was the only Israeli casualty of the raid. Another hostage, Doris Block, an elderly British citizen, had been taken to a hospital a few days before the rescue operation after she became ill. She was later murdered at Amin's behest. Shortly after the daring rescue made headlines, a television movie was made, "Raid on Entebbe," starring Yaphet Kotto and Charles Bronson.

Designed by Israeli artist Buky S. Schwartz, the *Jonathan Netanyahu Memorial* was dedicated October 16, 1986. Former Israeli prime minister Benjamin Netanyahu, who at the time was Israel's ambassador to the United Nations, was the keynote speaker at the dedication of the memorial to his older brother. The memorial committee was formed in 1980 by attorney Steven L. Friedman, a classmate of Jonathan Netanyahu's at Cheltenham High School in Wyncote, Pennsylvania, class of 1964.

Location: Congregation Mikveh Israel, 4th Street between Arch and Market streets.

Living Flame (Police and Firefighters) Memorial

Every occupation comes with its hazards, but some are clearly more hazardous than others, as visitors to the *Living Flame Memorial* in Franklin Square are silently urged to remember. A blue and white urn capped with a clear plastic flame and mounted upon a red tripod holds solemn vigil for those police and firefighters who made the ultimate sacrifice. Dedicated in 1976, the Living Flame is the site of annual ceremonies commemorating the fallen heroes, the names of whom are inscribed on stones surrounding the small plaza in which the structure stands. A plaque also lists police officers killed in the line of duty from 1828 to 1909, as well as firefighters from 1875 to 1888. Each column contains twenty-four names.

Reginald E. Beauchamp, who designed the *Living Flame Memorial*, was a businessman by vocation, and an artist by avocation. Very active both in professional and civic circles, he worked for thirty years as a newspaper executive for the *Philadelphia Bulletin*. His other creations include a large Plexiglas® bust of Benjamin Franklin, which was layered with some 80,000 pennies given by area school students, the *Whispering Bells of Freedom* memorial to Boston Massacre victim Crispus Attucks—located in front of the African American Museum at 7th and Arch streets, a *Vietnam War Memorial* for the city's Edison High School, and nearly two dozen other local commissions. His bust of Connie Mack—who managed the Philadelphia Athletics from 1901 to 1951—is in the Baseball Hall of Fame in Cooperstown, New York. Born in London in 1910, Beauchamp came to the United States when he was two. He died in 2000 at the age of ninety.

 **Location:** Franklin Square, 6th and Race streets.

The *Living Flame Memorial* by Reginald Beauchamp commemorates police and firefighters killed in the line of duty. *Photo courtesy of Stan Horwitz.*

View of *Religious Liberty* sculpture in front of the museum's glass façade © Jeff Goldberg/Esto, *Photo courtesy of National Museum of American Jewish History.*

Religious Liberty

Created for Philadelphia's Centennial International Exhibition in 1876, this monument was relocated from Fairmount Park to its current location, and rededicated, in 1986. The sculptor was Sir Jacob Moses Ezekiel. The central figure in this marble group is eight feet tall, and her left hand rests on the Constitution. The smaller, naked man to her right represents Religion, and carries in one hand the Torch of Faith. To the lady's left is an eagle seizing a serpent in its claws, symbolizing America's victory over tyranny.

 Location: National Museum of American Jewish History, 5th and Market streets.

The Liberty Bell

Inscribed on the front and center of the Liberty Bell, the words "PASS AND STOW" assume particular significance when one considers the history of this 259 year old American artifact. Made in London in 1751, the one-ton bell was removed numerous times from its intended perch in the state house steeple and placed in storage, for brief and extended periods. When first rung in 1753, the bell cracked and was taken down to be recast. This seemingly accomplished, the bell was subsequently reinstated, again removed, and again recast. During the Revolutionary War, the bell was spirited out of the city and hidden in an Allentown church, lest the British melt it down for munitions. In 1828, the bell collected dust while the city debated plans to dispose of it. These plans, of course, never came to fruition. In 1915, the Liberty Bell traveled across the country, headed for the Panama-Pacific Exposition in San Francisco, and was received like a celebrity at every stopover along the way.

However, "pass" and "stow" are not verbs in this case, but the surnames of two men named John, Philadelphians who twice recast the Liberty Bell, both times to the dissatisfaction of city officials. Apparently, the ringing produced cacophonous results. A new bell was finally ordered from the foundry in London, but the old bell was not discarded. The Liberty Bell sounded many times over the next century—to announce important meetings, rally support for political causes, celebrate the birthdays of presidents, and toll for the death of prominent individuals. The bell rang so many times that some city residents began to complain (Independence Hall Association).

The Liberty Bell shows evidence of wear around the frayed perimeter of the lip as well as the famous crack. Other, smaller fractures exist. The crack that rendered the bell mute, so to speak, came after a ringing in February 1846, for George Washington's birthday. In 2001, the bell sustained minor damage from a crazed tourist wielding a hammer.

The Liberty Bell is most often associated with the American Revolution, but obviously predates the war. The inscription on the crown, a verse from Leviticus 25:10, reads "PROCLAIM LIBERTY THROUGHOUT THE LAND AND UNTO ALL THE INHABITANTS THEREOF," which would naturally suggest the name *Liberty Bell*. But this nomenclature was first used in 1839 by an abolitionist group. Originally it was known simply as the State House Bell, and was ordered by the Pennsylvania Assembly, as the inscription beneath the Biblical verse attests.

Location: Liberty Bell Center, Market Street between 5th and 6th streets.

The Liberty Bell was first cast in England in 1751. The name Liberty Bell was first used in 1839 by an abolitionist group. *Photo courtesy of Peter J. Obst.*

The Whispering Bells of Freedom
(Memorial to Crispus Attucks)

These thirteen "whispering bells"—one bell for each colony—are so named because they have no clappers, the apparatuses that make bells ring. Installed in 1976, this memorial to slain sailor Crispus Attucks was designed by Reginald Beauchamp, who also designed the Living Flame Memorial (for fallen police and firefighters) at 6th and Race streets. The inscription for the *Whispering Bells of Freedom* reads: "The whispering bells of freedom / in honor of Crispus Attucks / who on March 5 1770 was killed by British troops / in Boston while protesting conditions / under the crown / These whispers of freedom grew into the crescendo of / The Declaration of Independence and the first ringing / of the Liberty Bell for independence."

Attucks was a former slave who was killed during the Boston Massacre, which occurred on the evening of March 5, 1770, in front of the Customs House in Boston when British troops fired into a mob of colonists. A lone British sentry, Hugh White, had called for assistance from his fellow soldiers after being harassed by an increasingly hostile crowd. After being taunted, then pelted with stones, snowballs and clubs, several of the British opened fire. The first of five to die in the incident, Attucks has been called a patriotic martyr whose status as a former slave added significance to his struggle for freedom, and a belligerent instigator who led a protest that escalated into deadly violence. The four other victims were Patrick Carr, Samuel Maverick, James Caldwell, and Samuel Gray. Attucks, Caldwell, and Gray died instantly; Carr and Maverick succumbed later from their injuries. Six others were wounded but survived.

Paul Revere made a famous engraving of the Boston Massacre, which at the time he referred to as "the bloody massacre perpetrated in King Street." Revere's engraving, the details of which were "borrowed" from another printer, was far from an accurate representation. Its main objective, however, was to further fuel anti-British sentiment, which was already swelling due to recently-imposed taxes on the Colonies and the large presence of British troops in Boston. Twelve British soldiers, including a captain, were arrested following the shooting. Two were eventually convicted of murder, and as punishment, were branded with the letter "M" (for "murder") on their right thumbs (Boston Massacre Historical Society).

Location: African American Museum, 7th and Arch streets.

The Whispering Bells of Freedom, by Reginald Beauchamp, is a tribute to slain sailor Crispus Attucks, killed during the Boston Massacre. *Photo courtesy of Stan Horwitz.*

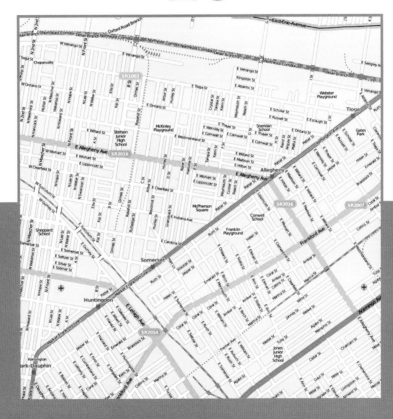

Charles Allen Smith

Sculpted by Francis P. Moitz, this memorial was erected in 1917 by the Allied Monument Committee of Philadelphia, one day short of the three-year anniversary of the death of its subject, a Kensington native. A sailor, Smith was killed at Vera Cruz, Mexico, in April 1914, during a United States occupation of the city. He left behind his parents—who were separated at the time—and his fiancée, whom he was to wed in October of that year. The press reported that two other Philadelphians, George D. Poinsett of Kensington and Elmer G. Rickerd of South Philadelphia, were also killed. Originally, a huge public funeral was planned for all three.

A tribute ceremony was held on May 13 at the Brooklyn Navy Yard for Poinsett and Smith, after which their remains were taken by train to Philadelphia for a grand burial procession. Two years after Smith's death, Kensington residents began raising funds for a memorial to the slain sailor. He was officially listed as the second of seventeen Americans killed during the engagement at Vera Cruz.

The chaos spawned by Mexico's Civil War precipitated the bloodshed at Vera Cruz. The already-tense situation was exacerbated when the country's newly elected leader, who had ousted the former dictator, was himself deposed by another dictator, General Victorio Huerta. The United States, long concerned with American interests in the region, once more had cause for alarm. Upon learning of a German munitions shipment bound for Vera Cruz, President Woodrow Wilson ordered U.S. naval forces stationed nearby to invade the port city and seize the weapons. This was accomplished in two days, with Mexican casualties about five times that of American losses.

Location: McPherson Square Park, Indiana Avenue and E Street, Kensington.

Francis P. Moitz's statue depicts a boy-faced Charles Allen Smith. *Photo courtesy of Roman Blazic.*

A panoramic view of McPherson Square Park. The *Charles Allen Smith Memorial* can be partially glimpsed on the right, behind a tree. *Photo courtesy of Roman Blazic.*

Don Quixote de la Mancha

Delivered in 1996, installed in November 1997, and dedicated the following month, this fourteen-foot, six-and-a-half-ton bronze depicts the hapless knight-errant astride his horse, Rozinante, whose head is thrown back in a nervous whinny. Clad in a breastplate but sans helmet, Don Quixote brandishes a lance in his right hand and holds a buckler in the other. Horse and rider rest atop an eight-foot granite base. An inscription in Spanish explains that this statue is a replica of an original—by sculptor Joaquin Garcia Donaire—in Ciudad Real, Spain, and a gift from the Spanish city to Philadelphia. In addition to being a token of friendship between sister cities, Donaire's dramatic sculpture was meant to inspire a developing South Kensington neighborhood, specifically one that was designated as an Empowerment Zone (Yant), an area in which businesses are given significant tax breaks to spur economic development.

Don Quixote was published in two parts, in 1605 and 1615. The goal of Spanish author Miguel de Cervantes (1547–1616) was not, as many readers assume, to satirize chivalry and knighthood, *per se*. Rather, he intended to take aim at the surfeit of tales, many of inferior quality, with which the reading public was enthralled (Campbell: 222). This he does masterfully, if unmercifully. The protagonist is a delusional old man who has literally gone mad from reading stories about knights-errant, so much so that he believes that he is one. Calling himself Don Quixote, he sets off on a series of adventures, accompanied by his chubby, dim-witted "squire" Sancho Panza. Determined to right wrongs and mete out justice wherever goes, Don Quixote battles windmills, interferes in the affairs of everyday people he encounters, and nearly gets himself and his sidekick killed on numerous occasions. Still, for all of the insult and injury to which the old man is subjected, he is an admirable, even heroic, figure.

Location: 2nd Street and Girard Avenue.

Don Quixote de la Mancha. This statue is a replica of an original in Ciudad Real, Spain. *Photo courtesy of Roman Blazic.*

Harrowgate Park War Memorial

This memorial, designed by Amelie Zell Felton, was dedicated in 1952. It was commissioned by the Harrowgate Park Civic Association.

Location: Harrowgate Park, Kensington Avenue and Tioga Street.

This memorial was commissioned by the Harrowgate Park Civic Association.
Photo courtesy of Roman Blazic.

William Penn and
Indian Land Commemorative

The most natural, and arguably most appropriate monument to mark the spot of William Penn's (1644–1718) 1682 Treaty of Peace and Amity with the Native American tribes was a stately elm. Known as "the Treaty Elm," this impressive tree effectively served the purpose until being uprooted in an 1810 storm. In 1827, the Penn Society erected an obelisk near the spot where the elm tree stood, on what was then private property. The slightly-faded inscriptions on all four sides of the obelisk are identical: TREATY GROUND / OF / WILLIAM PENN / AND THE / INDIAN NATIONS / 1682 / UNBROKEN FAITH. Even by 1827, the last part of the inscription no longer held true.

In 1893, Penn Treaty Park was established. Nearly a century later, a second manmade monument graced the treaty grounds—Frank C. Gaylord's William Penn statue. Sculpted from a huge block of Vermont granite, this 1983 installation was intended for the Pennsylvania tercentenary (1683–1983). Following a 1987 expansion of the park, yet another structure was added to the collection, the Indian Land Commemorative or the Treaty Monument. Artist Bob Hazous won a national competition. His piece is comprised of two eight-by-twelve-foot sheets of steel, placed parallel and mounted on a concrete base. Looming like an enormous, perforated, rusty plane, this $60,000 acquisition is set back from the park.

The site of the legendary treaty was known as Shackamaxon—a settlement along the banks of the Delaware River in what is now the Kensington section of the city. The treaty is described as "legendary" because no official documentation exists. Nevertheless, this historic event has been depicted by artists many times, most famously by painter Benjamin West in 1772. Tamanend represented the Indian tribes at this historic event.

Location: Penn Treaty Park, Delaware Avenue and Marlborough Street.

William Penn, Penn Treaty Park. *Photo courtesy of Roman Blazic.*

The old obelisk in Penn Treaty Park. *Photo courtesy of Roman Blazic.*

The Indian Land Commemorative, by Bob Hazous. *Photo courtesy of Roman Blazic.*

Andrey Sheptytsky

Currently a candidate for beatification in the Ukrainian Greco-Catholic Church, Andrey Sheptytsky (1865–1944) chose a life of service and humility rather than the wealth and privilege into which he was born. The son of Ukrainian nobles, Sheptytsky was a count, but took monastic orders in 1891, against the wishes of his father. A decade later he was made Metropolitan of Lviv. A *cause célèbre* of Sheptytsky's was the reconciliation of the Orthodox and Catholic churches, which have been at odds since a 1054 schism.

A miracle attributed to Sheptytsky concerns the fulfilling of a prediction that he made shortly before his death in November of 1944: the Ukrainian Greco-Catholic Church would be dissolved, but eventually reborn. Two years later, the Russian Orthodox Church, coerced by Soviet authorities, essentially absorbed the Ukrainian Greco-Catholic Church, forcing the faithful underground for decades, until the fall of the Soviet Union (Metropolitan Andrey Sheptytksy Institute).

Inscriptions on the base of this statue are in Ukrainian and English.

Location: Ukrainian Catholic Cathedral of the Immaculate Conception, Franklin Street between Brown and Poplar streets.

"Andrei (Andrew) Sheptytksy / Metropolitan of Halych, Ukraine / July 29, 1865 / November 1, 1944."
Photo courtesy of Teresa Siwak.

Benjamin Franklin and His Kite

Although many of Benjamin Franklin's experiments seemed whimsical at the time, nearly all evolved into practical applications and inventions. This 1965 sculpture by Agnes Yarnall was originally placed at the Franklin Institute Research Laboratories at 20th and Race streets, and commemorates Franklin's most famous experiment—a daring, dangerous exercise involving a kite, a key, and a thunderstorm. After waiting for "perfect" weather, Franklin flew a kite as high as he could, watching the distant diamond buffeted by the wind. Assisting Franklin was his son, William. (Later the two men would forever part ways due to a disagreement on the issue of American independence.) At the base of the kite string Franklin tied a key, to which he in turn tied a ribbon to prevent his being electrocuted. After a while, the two men's efforts were rewarded when an electrical charge frizzled Franklin's eager fingers. This eventually lead to Franklin's invention of the lightning rod.

Two misconceptions arose from Franklin's forays into electricity. The first is that Franklin discovered electricity. In fact, scientists had been aware of electricity for some time, and had conducted their own experiments using rudimentary "electric tubes." What Franklin did was verify his theory that lightning was electricity. The second common fallacy is that lightning rods prevent lightning from striking a building, when they simply ground the electricity so that the structure in question is not damaged.

Location: Coxe Park, Cherry Street between 21st and 22nd streets.

Benjamin Franklin and His Kite, 1965 by Agnes Yarnall. *Photo courtesy of Stan Horwitz.*

Roberto Clemente

Behind a statue of Roberto Clemente in a North Philadelphia school yard, a plaque on a brick wall bears a quote, in both Spanish and English, from the baseball Hall-of-Famer. The words are sadly prophetic: "I want to be remembered as someone that gave all he had to give." On New Year's Eve, 1972, Clemente did just that, dying in an airplane crash while supervising the delivery of relief supplies to Managua, Nicaragua, following a deadly earthquake. His body was never recovered. Clemente left behind a wife, Vera, three sons, and millions of bereaved fans.

Clemente was and remains an inspiration and source of pride for the Hispanic community, as much for his activism as for his athleticism. An outspoken opponent of racism, he had a contentious relationship with the press, who frequently ridiculed his accent and command of the English language (Smithsonian). From 1954 to 1955, Clemente spent an uneventful season with the minor league Montreal Royals. The following year he signed with the Pittsburgh Pirates, with whom he would stay for the remainder of his career. Both in the batter's cage and in the field, Clemente was a star player. He scored 3,000 career hits, 240 of which were home runs, and in 1966 was named the National League Most Valuable Player (MVP). Clemente was the first Hispanic to be inducted into the Hall of Fame.

On September 15, 1997, a seven-foot, half-ton statue of the late Pirates right-fielder was unveiled in the courtyard of the middle school bearing his name. Students, staff, and community members thought that the memorial was a welcome addition to the new school building, which two years prior had replaced a dilapidated warehouse. Philadelphia sculptor Phil Sumpter, who later created the Negro Leagues

Roberto Clemente was, and remains, an inspiration and source of pride for the Hispanic community, as much for his activism as for his athleticism. *Photo courtesy of David Cruz/Al Dia News.*

Memorial at Belmont and Parkside avenues, depicted Clemente in full swing mode after connecting with the baseball. Clemente stands on a four-inch granite base shaped like his native Puerto Rico. The nearly $100,000 cost for the memorial was raised through private and corporate donations, as well as grant money.

Location: Roberto Clemente Middle School courtyard, Front Street and Erie Avenue.

Stephen Girard

In front of Founder's Hall at Girard College stands a statuary group depicting the school's namesake surrounded by a diverse group of children. From the top tier of an uniquely shaped pedestal, Stephen Girard looks down benevolently at the youth, while they in turn gaze up at him almost reverently. The memorial was dedicated on May 20th, 2000. The sculptor was Bruno Lucchesi, who throughout his long career has executed over fifty public commissions in America and his native Italy.

Although his philanthropic side cannot be ignored, Stephen Girard is probably best remembered as the ultimate capitalist. Born in Bordeaux, France, in 1750, he arrived in Philadelphia in 1776, already an experienced sailor who had spent half his boyhood at sea. Girard remained in Philadelphia for the remainder of his life, and amassed a fortune in the mercantile shipping and banking businesses. In 1811, Girard purchased the Bank of the United States for $1.2 million after the bank's charter expired. He then privately operated the bank, which at the time of his death was estimated to hold $5 million in assets (NewsBank).

During Philadelphia's Yellow Fever plague of 1793, which wiped out one in ten residents, Girard helped minister to the afflicted at the city's Bush Hill Hospital. A December 5, 1793, article in the *National Gazette*, referring to a visit to the hospital by Dr. George Logan, stated: "the sick are well accommodated, and every attention given to render their situation easy and comfortable by citizens Gerard [sic] and Holme."

A childless widower nearing the end of his life, Girard made out his will, with a bequest calling for an institution that provided a free education for impoverished white male orphans. This stipulation was eventually challenged and subsequently overturned in 1968, and today there are no restrictions based on race or gender. Girard died in 1831, and the school opened seventeen years later.

Location: Girard College, Girard and Corinthian avenues.

From the top tier of a uniquely shaped pedestal, Stephen Girard looks down benevolently at the youth, while they in turn gaze up at him almost reverently. *Photo courtesy of Tatiana Heller.*

Founder's Hall, Girard College. *Photo courtesy of Tatiana Heller.*

"THE SPIRIT OF GIRARD"
Sculpture by Bruno Lucchesi

Gift of the Class of June, 1937

Dedicated Founder's Day
May 20, 2000
The 250th Anniversary
Of the Birth of the Founder

*Symbolizing the timeless spirit of Stephen Girard
And his unshakable belief in success
Through education and motivation*

The dedicatory plaque. *Photo courtesy of Tatiana Heller.*

Over the Top

This 1920 sculpture by John Paulding commemorates the American infantry soldiers of World War I, who were known as "doughboys." The inscription on the front of the base reads "IN MEMORY OF / OUR BOYS / OF THE SIXTH, / ELEVENTH AND / TWELFTH WARDS / WHO SERVED / IN THE / GREAT WAR / OF THE NATIONS / 1914–1918."

Location: 2nd and Spring Garden streets.

Over the Top, 1920. *Photo courtesy of Tatiana Heller.*

Penn's Landing 13

Columbus Monument

The *Columbus Monument* on a clear day. *Photo courtesy of Venturi, Scott Brown and Associates, Inc.*

The drive for the erection of a monument commemorating the 500th anniversary of the voyage of Christopher Columbus was spearheaded by a group calling itself America 500 Anniversary Corp., who enlisted Philadelphia architect Robert Venturi for the task. Incorporating both conventional and abstract elements, this monument consists of a stylized obelisk, 106 feet high, constructed of steel panels over a steel framework, which have the appearance of segmented wedges stacked eight high, not counting the capstone. The gaps between the overlying steel panels are sixteen inches. The surmounting banner incorporates the colors of the flags of Italy and Spain, and also functions as a weathervane. The structure occupies the center of a plaza in the shape of a compass rose. The total cost was just over one million dollars (VSBA).

Plans for the Columbus monument were met with a mixture of nationalistic pride, gloomy cynicism, and plain indifference. Supporters emphasized what critics condemned about the legacy of the Genoan sailor—he paved the way for European exploration and colonization of the New World. The organizers tried to downplay any political ramifications.

The grand unveiling came on the evening of Sunday, October 11, 1992, following a weekend of festivities capped off by a huge parade. Starting from JFK Plaza at 15th and Arch streets, the parade proceeded northwest up the Benjamin Franklin Parkway towards the Art Museum, wound counterclockwise around Eakins Oval, then headed back down the Parkway to where it began. Opera singer Luciano Pavarotti, riding in a horse-drawn carriage, served as the grand marshal. As 50,000 observers watched, some 7,000 marched in what was billed as the largest Columbus Day Parade in the world.

The grandiose celebration did not go off entirely without a hitch. Several protesters dressed in Native American garb splattered the monument with red paint, then fled in their vehicle.

Location: Columbus Boulevard and Dock Street, Penn's Landing.

Philadelphia Beirut Memorial

On the morning of October 23, 1983, a suicide bomber drove a truck laden with explosives into the Marine barracks in Beirut, Lebanon. The devastating blast that ensued claimed the lives of 241 servicemen and injured dozens of others. The Marines had been deployed as part of a peace keeping force due to tensions between sectarian elements within Lebanon. Hezbollah was suspected in the deadly attack, but denied responsibility. The Beirut bombing bore eerie similarities to a terrorist incident six months earlier, when a suicide bomber with the same modus operandi killed sixty-three people at the U.S. Embassy in Beirut, nearly a third of them Americans (PBS).

In May of 1985, families of the nine Philadelphia-area Marines killed in the Beirut bombing started campaigning for a memorial to their loved ones, who ranged in age from nineteen to twenty-nine. Within five months their plan came to fruition with the Sunday, October 20, dedication of a bronze and granite structure featuring an eagle atop a globe with an anchor. Beneath this globe is a stone with a memorial plaque listing the names of the young men who died. The cost was $20,000.

Location: Front and Spruce streets, Penn's Landing.

The *Philadelphia Beirut Memorial*, 1985 by Douglas Corsini. *Photo courtesy of Stan Horwitz.*

Philadelphia Korean War Memorial

Wedged ingloriously between World War II and Vietnam, the three-year "police action" in Korea has been dubbed "the Forgotten War." Following a communist invasion of South Korea on June 25, 1950, a United Nations force comprised of sixteen nations resolved to repulse the unprovoked attack. U.S. forces bore the brunt of the fighting. The aging veterans of the conflict have been trying to counter America's ignorance regarding a struggle that claimed the lives of some 54,000 U.S. troops. On June 22, 2002, they had a small measure of success with the dedication of Philadelphia's *Korean War Memorial*.

Six sixteen-foot black granite walls surrounding four columns in the center of a plaza form the mainstay of the memorial. Etched into the walls are images, maps, and detailed text describing the different phases of the Korean War. A column with a Purple Heart emblem at the top lists the names of the 610 Philadelphia-area veterans killed in action, and categorized according to the years that they died (1950–1953). One newspaper reporter described the exhibit as an "elaborate, colorful Korean history-book-in-stone" (Goldwyn). Four memorial plaques were later placed at the site, featuring tributes to nurses who served during the Korean War and to Marines killed in World War II, Korea, and Vietnam, a letter from former South Korean president Kim Dae-jung, and an emblem of the Korean War Veterans Association. Ground was broken in 1999. The project was funded by city and state grant money, as well as private donations. On October 7, 2006, the memorial was rededicated.

Location: 38th Parallel Place, Foglietta Plaza, Penn's Landing.

Philadelphia's *Korean War Memorial. Photo courtesy of Stan Horwitz.*

Philadelphia Vietnam Veterans Memorial

The official dates for what was arguably the most controversial war in which the United States was involved vary depending on the source. As the start of the conflict, some cite 1964, during the Gulf of Tonkin incident. Others say 1965, when the first U.S. combat troops arrived. American military advisors were in Vietnam as early as 1959. But the general consensus is that the Fall of Saigon in 1975 was the official end.

By 1987, Philadelphia finally had its own Vietnam memorial, acknowledging the many Philadelphians who served in the protracted conflict, and in particular the 646 who made the ultimate sacrifice. The Philadelphia memorial bears some similarity to the one in Washington, D.C. in that both feature names inscribed on a granite wall. Philadelphia's memorial, however, has two walls: a semi-circular one engraved with the names of the 646 Philadelphians killed in action, and an opposing straight wall depicting chronological events from the Vietnam War. To the left of the granite panels depicting the chronology of the war are engraved the insignia of the five service branches—Army, Navy, Air Force, Marines, and Coast Guard—as well as a world map, and to the right, a map of Southeast Asia. At the center of the plaza formed by the two walls is a depiction of an eagle with dog tags in its beak, and superimposed over the Liberty Bell. Annual Memorial Day ceremonies are held at the site.

The winning design for a 1985 contest was submitted by architect Perry M. Morgan, and was chosen from among 102 entries. The competition was limited to those residing within fifty miles of the city. Overseeing the memorial was a panel of seven, four of whom were Vietnam combat veterans. This was to preclude any controversy similar to that which arose in the wake of Maya Lin's design for the Wall in Washington, D.C. (Philadelphia Vietnam Veterans Memorial). In

Philadelphia's *Vietnam Veterans Memorial*. The winning design for a 1985 contest was submitted by architect Perry M. Morgan, and was chosen from among 102 entries. *Photo courtesy of Stan Horwitz.*

1984, Philadelphia Mayor Wilson Goode had signed a bill authorizing the establishment of a memorial fund.

In recent years, security cameras have been installed at the memorial to deter vandalism.

Location: Front and Spruce streets, Penn's Landing.

Tamanend

This twenty-two-and-a-half-foot bronze sculpture, dedicated in 1995, depicts the Leni-Lenape Indian who signed the famous treaty with William Penn at Shackamaxon in 1682. The turtle under Tamanend's feet represents the earth, while an eagle carrying a wampum belt perches on his left shoulder. The sculptor was Raymond Sandoval.

Location: Front and Market streets.

Tamanend, 1995 by Raymond Sandoval. *Photo courtesy of Roman Blazic.*

The Irish Memorial

Tinged with tragedy, the *Irish Memorial* in Philadelphia depicts the haggard faces of thirty-five men, women, and children plodding across a bleak bronze landscape to eventually disembark onto a new land. But for all its pathos, Glenna C. Goodacre's thirty-foot by twelve-foot by twelve-foot masterpiece radiates courage, promise, and the resilience of a generation of proud people.

The massive bronze sculpture group, which was cast at a Denver, Colorado foundry commemorates the 150th anniversary of the Great Irish Potato Famine, which claimed one million lives between 1845 and 1850. Crop disease wiped out the staple diet of most Irish in the mid-nineteenth century. The British, who ruled Ireland at the time, have been condemned for their apathy towards the plight of the poor, particularly because the wealthy British landowners shipped a lot of food out of the country. This resulted in a huge exodus from the Emerald Isle to the more promising shores of America. Boatloads of impoverished immigrants sought opportunity in urban centers on the East Coast, particularly around the Boston, Massachusetts, area. But most found life difficult on the other side of the Atlantic as well, meeting with suspicion and outright hostility. Negative stereotypes dogged them in their search for work and lodging. Still they persevered, proving themselves to be industrious and productive members of society. Today, over forty million Americans claim Irish heritage.

Goodacre, who designed the *Women's Vietnam Memorial* on the Mall in Washington, D.C. and the golden Sacagawea one-dollar coin, was awarded the commission in 1997. After the Irish Memorial was modeled in Goodacre's Santa Fe, New Mexico studio the piece was cast at a foundry in

The massive bronze sculpture group commemorates the 150th anniversary of the Great Irish Potato Famine, which claimed one million lives between 1845 and 1850. *Photo courtesy of Stan Horwitz.*

Denver, Colorado, and shipped by truck to Philadelphia. The three million dollar memorial was unveiled in November of 2002, and officially opened to the public the following October. The surrounding one-and-three-quarter-acre park was designed by landscape architect Pauline Hurley-Kurtz.

Location: Southeast corner of Front and Chestnut streets, Penn's Landing.

Rittenhouse Square 14

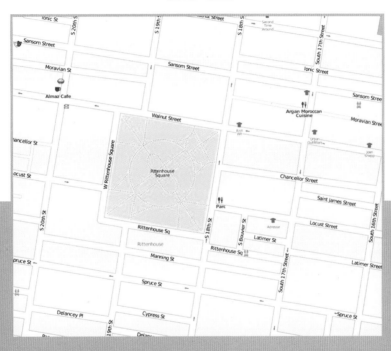

Evelyn Taylor Price Memorial

This tribute was created by Philadelphian Beatrice Fenton in memory of Price, who was president of the Rittenhouse Square Improvement Association—which commissioned the sundial—and the Rittenhouse Square Flower Market Committee.

Location: Southwest corner of 18th and Walnut streets.

This tribute was created by Philadelphian Beatrice Fenton in memory of Price. *Photo courtesy of Tatiana Heller.*

Roxborough 15

21ˢᵗ Ward War Memorial

A stone eagle perches on a stone ball atop this memorial, which features an alcove whose ceiling is filled with gold stars. On the lower part of the alcove wall are inscribed names. Tuscan columns flank the alcove. Inscribed beneath the perched eagle reads "To the memory of the boys from the 21ˢᵗ Ward who lost their lives in the World War 1914–1918." Under a ledge beneath that inscriptions read "KOREAN WORLD WAR II VIETNAM." The memorial was originally dedicated on November 13, 1920. The approximate cost was $13,000.

Location: Gorgas Park, Ridge Avenue and Hermitage Street.

The *21ˢᵗ Ward War Memorial*. Photo courtesy of Stan Horwitz.

Christopher Columbus

While sculptor Emanuele Caroni may have aimed for a serious or even haughty demeanor, his marble Christopher Columbus seems to glare from atop his pedestal. The explorer's right hand rests on top of a globe. An inscription beneath him reads "Presented to the city of Philadelphia by the Italian citizens / In commemoration of the first centenary American Independence 1876." The dedication was held on Columbus Day. Depicted in relief on the pedestal are scenes from the voyage of Columbus, as well as the seals of both Italy and the United States. The cost of this monument was about $18,000.

Whether or not Christopher Columbus (1451–1506) discovered the New World is hotly debated; strong arguments support earlier arrivals by Scandinavians, and Native Americans are thought to have migrated from Asia over 10,000 years ago. What is generally agreed is that the Genoese sailor opened the floodgates for European colonization. For several years Columbus solicited King Ferdinand and Queen Isabella of Spain to finance his quest for a shorter sailing route to China. In 1492 the royal pair finally acquiesced. With the ships, the *Nina*, *Pinta*, and *Santa Maria*, Columbus and his crew landed at San Salvador on October 12, after about nine weeks at sea. Between then and 1502, Columbus made a total of four voyages across the Atlantic. Throughout his maritime sojourns, Columbus was frequently incorrect about where he landed and how far he had gone. He dubbed the Native Americans "Indians" because he thought that he had reached India. Columbus Day was celebrated in America in 1892, the 400th anniversary of the culmination of the first voyage, after President Benjamin Harrison issued a proclamation (Library of Congress).

Location: Marconi Plaza, West side of Broad Street and South of Oregon Avenue.

Christopher Columbus. 1876 by Emanuele Caroni. *Photo courtesy of Roman Blazic.*

Guglielmo Marconi

Guglielmo Marconi (1874–1937) was born in Bologna, Italy, to an Italian father and an Irish mother. Like most inventors and pioneers in their respective fields, he manifested an interest and an aptitude in physics and related subjects from an early age. His experiments with telegraphy grew more sophisticated and successful, commencing with an 1895 endeavor at his father's estate in which he succeeded in sending a signal over a mile, and culminating with a 2,000-plus mile signal, from Cornwall, England, to Newfoundland, Canada, just six years later. Marconi worked feverishly over the next decade, patenting several inventions. In 1909 he shared the Nobel Prize for Physics with German scientist Ferdinand Braun. Optimistic about continued advancement in his field, Marconi stated in his Nobel lecture, delivered on December 11, 1909:

> Whatever may be its present shortcomings and defects, there can be no doubt that wireless telegraphy—even over great distances—has come to stay, and not only stay, but continue to advance (Nobelprize.org).

Marconi's title of "the Father of Wireless Telegraphy" is disputed by some, who feel that Russian scientist Alexander Popov (1859–1906) is at least as deserving of that honor.

Designed by Giancarlo Saleppichi, this memorial to Marconi was dedicated in 1975.

Location: Marconi Plaza, east side of Broad Street and south of Oregon Avenue.

The top inscription reads: GUGLIELMO MARCONI / INVENTOR WIRELESS TELEGRAPHY / THE FATHER OF / MODERN COMMUNICATIONS / APRIL 25, 1874 / JULY 20, 1937.
The bottom inscription reads: ERECTED BY / THE CITY OF PHILADELPHIA / UNDER THE LEADERSHIP OF / FRANK L. RIZZO. MAYOR / AND THE ITALO-AMERICAN COMMUNITY / ORGANIZED AS THE MARCONI MEMORIAL / ASSOCIATION INCORPORATED / FRANK P. DIDIO. M.D. PRESIDENT / DEDICATED NOVEMBER 4, 1979. *Photo courtesy of Roman Blazic.*

Walt Whitman

This statue of the poet Walt Whitman was made from a 1939 cast by sculptor Jo Davidson. The original is in New York. In 1957, Davidson's Whitman was installed at the Broad Street and Packer Avenue site, and officially dedicated two years later.

Whitman has been labeled arrogant, indolent, unconventional, and uncompromising. The first two charges were possibly true, the third and fourth certainly were. His unorthodox style of poetry—which eschewed the use of both meter and rhyme—isolated Whitman from some of the stodgier traditionalists, but endeared him to free thinkers such as Ralph Waldo Emerson and Henry David Thoreau. His most famous work, *Leaves of Grass*, was originally self-published in 1855, and later revised and expanded throughout several printings. As an unofficial volunteer "nurse," Whitman spent much of his time ministering to wounded soldiers during the Civil War, and he was profoundly affected by what he witnessed. This led to his publication of *Drum-Taps* (1865), in which he included his most famous poem "When Lilacs Last in the Dooryard Bloom'd," which dealt with the assassination of President Lincoln. Whitman's work was too candid for some sensibilities, drawing accusations of lewdness. He frequently alluded to his own latent homosexuality.

After a disabling stroke in 1873, the fifty-one-year-old Whitman went to live with his brother George in Camden, New Jersey. While Whitman was close to his brother, whom he had visited after the latter was wounded during his Civil War service, George was not his intellectual equal. As a result, Whitman grew bored and discouraged (Baym: 1967). Although Whitman lived nearly another two decades, he never fully regained his health. He died on March 26, 1892.

Location: Southwest corner of Broad Street and Packer Avenue, by the entrance to the Walt Whitman Bridge.

This statue of the poet Walt Whitman was made from a 1939 cast by sculptor Jo Davidson. The original is in New York.
Photo courtesy of Roman Blazic.

Walt Whitman

A second memorial to nineteenth century poet Walt Whitman, also in South Philadelphia, stands at 4th Street and Oregon Avenue. Artist Leonard Baskin seems to have been a good choice for the Whitman commission, given Baskin's affinity for the written word and his experience in the field of publishing; he founded Gehenna Press in 1942 while a student at Yale University, and his literary efforts resulted in books on diverse subjects such as zoology, folklore, and natural history. As an artist, Baskin's creations ranged from woodcuts to watercolors to statuary. His first sculptural exhibition was in 1939 at the studio of Maurice Glickman, under whom the young Baskin studied for two years. Baskin later taught Art for twenty-one years at Smith College in Northampton, Massachusetts. He traveled to Europe on several occasions, studying in France and Italy, and lived in England for about ten years, after which he returned to the United States. Baskin then resumed teaching for another decade, this time at Hampshire College in Amherst, Massachusetts. Several large-scale projects came later in his career, including the Holocaust Memorial in Ann Arbor, Michigan, in 1994, and a bronze bas-relief for the Franklin Delano Roosevelt Memorial in Washington, D.C., in 1997. The former probably had special significance to Baskin, who was the son of a rabbi. Baskin died in 2000, at the age of seventy-seven.

Location: Whitman Plaza, 4th Street and Oregon Avenue.

Walt Whitman, by Leonard Baskin. *Photo courtesy of Stan Horwitz.*

Temple University 17

Johnnie Ring

During the Civil War, Johnnie Ring served as valet to Russell H. Conwell, who would later found Temple University. At the time of Ring's service, Conwell was a captain in the 46th Massachusetts Infantry. Ring died of burns received after he ran across a burning bridge to rescue a ceremonial sword from Conwell's tent following a Confederate attack.

Location: Mitten Hall, Temple University campus.

Johnnie Ring, 1964 by Boris Blai. *Photo courtesy of Stan Horwitz.*

Lincoln the Lawyer

Illinois license plates read "Land of Lincoln," and while the sixteenth president made a name for himself in that state, rural Kentucky was his birthplace. The son of illiterate farmers, Lincoln became a voracious reader, educating himself on a wide range of topics, eventually including law. His experiences as an itinerant attorney for the Illinois Eighth Circuit Court honed the skills he would later employ—albeit unsuccessfully—in his famous senate debates against the glib Stephen A. Douglas. At the time that he was sparring with Douglas, Lincoln had already served in the Illinois state legislature and in the house of representatives. A Republican, Lincoln was elected president in 1860, winning 40% of the vote. His Democratic opponent in the following election in 1864 was Civil War General George B. McClellan. Lincoln won handily, but at bitter cost.

This 1968 bust of *Lincoln the Lawyer* is by Emil Seletz.

Lincoln the Lawyer, 1968 by Emil Seletz. *Photo courtesy of Temple University Beasley School of Law.*

Location: Temple University Law School, Broad Street and Montgomery Avenue.

Russell Conwell

Philadelphia's largest university has its origins in a modest house of worship located at Berks and Mervine streets, where in 1884 a group of divinity students assembled weekly for tutoring. Instructing his young charges was Russell H. Conwell, Civil War veteran, lawyer, and most recently, pastor of Grace Baptist Church. So successful were Conwell's endeavors that a mere four years later, Temple College—which became Temple University in 1907—was issued a charter. Conwell served as both pastor of the church and president of the college until his death in 1925 at age eighty-two. Prior to his years in Philadelphia, Conwell had practiced law in Boston and worked as a journalist.

The author of over three dozen books on topics philosophical, biographical, historical, and spiritual, Conwell was also a superb educator, administrator, orator, and preacher, who in the latter capacity had no problem reconciling capitalism with Christianity. In his famous "Acres of Diamonds" speech, delivered literally thousands of times to audiences all over the world, Conwell emphasized the importance of obtaining wealth, particularly as a means of spreading good. The gist of the speech, however, was about the opportunities that are available to everyone close to home, and was inspired by a story that Conwell heard from a travel guide while sightseeing in Iran (then Persia) as a young man.

This 1968 bust of Conwell is by Russian sculptor Boris Blai, who four years earlier had completed the statue of Johnnie Ring (page 157). The inscription simply reads "Russell H. Conwell, Founder of Temple University, 1843–1925."

Location: Founder's Garden, Temple University campus.

RUSSELL H. CONWELL / FOUNDER OF / TEMPLE UNIVERSITY / 1843–1924 / BY BORIS BLAI.
Photo courtesy of Stan Horwitz.

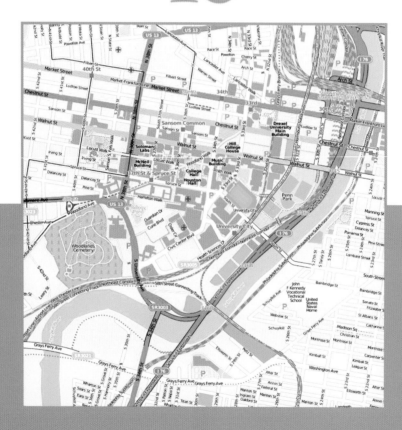

All Wars Memorial to Penn Alumni

The centerpiece of the *All Wars Memorial to Penn Alumni* is a two-and-a-half-ton bronze sculpture consisting of a large urn surrounded by five seven-foot bronze figures, male and female, who symbolize the "Unity of Man and Mutual Toleration" (Lloyd). The inscription on the accompanying wall reads: THE UNIVERSITY OF PENNSYLVANIA / 1740 TO HER SON WHO DIED IN THE SERVICE OF HER COUNTRY 1950 / A BROOD OF STURDY MEN WHO STOOD FOR FREEDOM AND TRUTH. SIR WALTER MITCHELL, CLASS OF 1848. Dedicated in November 1952, the *All Wars Memorial* was commissioned by Walter Annenberg.

Sculptor Charles Rudy was born in York, Pennsylvania, in 1904, where his father had a stained glass business. After living in New York for ten years, where he taught sculpture, Rudy moved to Bucks County, Pennsylvania. There he and his wife, Lorraine, purchased a farm and Rudy set up a studio. Rudy worked with a variety of media throughout his career, including scrap metal from his job at a factory where he was employed during the Second World War. In addition to Penn's *All Wars Memorial*, his major commissions include a large, marble Noah for the Bronx post office, the frieze on the Lehigh County (Pennsylvania) Courthouse, two bas-reliefs of Benjamin Franklin for the Pennsylvania/New Jersey bridge that bears that Founding Father's name, and the *Confederate War Memorial* on Stone Mountain in Georgia. The latter was a collaborative effort involving dozens of sculptors. Rudy died in 1986 in Doylestown, Pennsylvania.

Location: East side of 33rd Street, south of Walnut Street, across from Smith Walk.

Detail of the wall of the *All Wars Memorial to Penn Alumni*. Photo courtesy of Anna Jensky.

The *All Wars Memorial to Penn Alumni*. Photo courtesy of Anna Jensky.

One of many bronze Bens in Philadelphia. *Photo courtesy of Anna Jensky*.

Benjamin Franklin

In this unusual 1987 sculpture of Ben Franklin by George Lundeen, Franklin is seated on a modern bench, a pigeon perched on the other end. Franklin's right hand is resting on the top of his cane, while his left hand loosely holds the *Pennsylvania Gazette* that he is reading. Franklin's pose is casual, relaxed.

Location: University of Pennsylvania campus, 37th Street and Locust Walk.

Charles Lennig

Charles Lennig was the president of a large construction firm, and a generous donor to the University of Pennsylvania. This memorial bust was commissioned by his son, Nicholas. The sculptor was John J. Boyle, whose other pieces in Philadelphia include that of attorney and civic leader John Christian Bullitt at City Hall (1907) and Benjamin Franklin, also by College Hall on the Penn campus (1899). The unveiling of the Lennig memorial took place with little fanfare in late April 1891: the dedication was held several weeks later. The piece had been installed a year prior, but because of a flaw was kept inside during cold weather.

Nicholas Lennig died in January 1906, fifteen years after Charles. In his will, he left, among other bequests, $3,000 for the upkeep of his father's memorial.

Location: College Hall, University of Pennsylvania campus, 34th and Spruce streets.

This bust of Charles Lennig was given to the University of Pennsylvania by Lennig's son, Nicholas. *Photo courtesy of Anna Jensky.*

Clark Park Civil War Memorial. This dull gray stone, culled from the battlefield at Gettysburg, Pennsylvania, serves almost as a grave marker for the once proud army hospital that covered about twelve acres. *Photo courtesy of Stan Horwitz.*

Clark Park Civil War Memorial

This dull gray stone, culled from the battlefield at Gettysburg, Pennsylvania, serves almost as a grave marker for the once proud army hospital that covered about twelve acres. On the front of the pedestal is a modest plaque. Erected in 1916, the memorial hardly does justice to the legacy of what was the largest Union hospital during the Civil War. But what memorial could?

From 1862 to 1865, Satterlee Hospital treated thousands of sick and wounded soldiers, with surprisingly few patient deaths. Recently appointed U.S. Surgeon General William A. Hammond supervised construction of the new facility, which was originally called West Philadelphia U.S. General Hospital. In 1863 Hammond officially renamed the institution in honor of army surgeon Richard Satterlee, in recognition of his "faithful and meritorious services" (NewsBank). Isaac I. Hayes, who had served as ship's surgeon during an arctic expedition about a decade earlier, was placed in charge of the new hospital. The volunteer services of nuns from the Sisters of Charity proved invaluable in assisting doctors and staff, as well as the tens of thousands of men who passed through the hospital doors.

Satterlee fulfilled a need that rudimentary field hospitals could not, especially when it became apparent that the conflict would not be a quick one, a realization which came in the wake of the Federal defeat at First Bull Run (Clements: 4). Satterlee was in all respects a modern hospital, and operated with remarkable efficiency. Some of the major battles, however, severely taxed Satterlee's resources, in particular the wave of wounded following the July 1863, bloodbath at Gettysburg (ibid.: 21-22). But despite its exemplary record, Satterlee closed in August of 1865, and was gradually dismantled.

Location: Clark Park, Baltimore Avenue and 43rd Street.

Dickens and Little Nell

Sculpted by Francis Edwin Elwell, this seated bronze statue of the celebrated English author and a character from the novel *The Old Curiosity Shop* has been at its present location since 1902. For nearly four decades, the memorial has been the site of annual celebrations of Dickens' birthday, February 7. The sculpture was originally created for the 1893 World's Columbian Exhibition in Chicago. Afterwards, it was offered to Dickens' descendants as a gift, but they refused, citing the author's wish that no likeness of him be made. While this monument features the only known statue of Dickens, other statues of Little Nell were created, notably one by John Rogers. Elwell's *Dickens and Little Nell* was cast at a foundry in Philadelphia in 1890.

First published in weekly installments beginning in 1840, *The Old Curiosity Shop* tells the tale of Little Nell Trent and her grandfather, who reside in London and run the titular establishment. Unknown to young Nell, her grandfather has a serious gambling problem, which ruins his business and forces him to turn to Daniel Quilp, a ruthless moneylender. Quilp seizes the shop and ousts the proprietor and Nell, who become itinerant beggars. Even after evicting the pair, the merciless Quilp continues to hound them. Readers were saddened, then incensed, when Dickens killed off Little Nell.

Charles Dickens was born in 1812 in Portsea, Hampshire, England. When Dickens was a boy, his father spent three years in debtor's prison, which undoubtedly influenced the young Charles, whose later novels dealt with the inequities of nineteenth-century English society, particularly the gap between the rich and the poor. His writings probably did more to expose past injustices than remedy present ones, however. His more famous works include *A Christmas Carol*, *A Tale of Two Cities*, *Oliver Twist*, and *David Copperfield*. At the time of his death in 1870, Dickens was working on *Edwin Drood*.

Location: Clark Park, 43rd Street and Chester Avenue.

Dickens and Little Nell, 1902 by Francis Edwin Elwell. *Photo courtesy of Stan Horwitz.*

Edgar Fahs Smith

Edgar Fahs Smith. Photo courtesy of Anna Jensky.

Edgar Fahs Smith (1856–1928) was a chemistry professor at the University of Pennsylvania, and served as the school's vice-provost from 1899 to 1910, then as provost from 1911 to 1920. Educated in the United States and Europe, Smith held a PhD in chemistry when he began teaching at the University of Pennsylvania, and also received three honorary degrees from that institution. Smith was a serious writer, authoring numerous scientific books, as well as biographies of prominent chemists. He was a proactive and progressive administrator, whose sweeping changes to the university resulted in significant growth in the school's faculty, enrollment, and endowment. In particular he championed the cause of women in the sciences (University of Pennsylvania Archives and Records Center). His memorial, sculpted by R. Tait McKenzie, was sponsored by John C. Bell, an alumnus from the class of 1889. Atypically for a memorial, the Smith statue was installed while its subject was still alive, in 1925. Smith is depicted seated, wearing a gown, and holding a cap in his right hand. Behind his chair is a stack of books. At Smith's right foot, a lizard peeks inconspicuously from beneath the folds of the professor's gown.

The sculptor, McKenzie, also taught at the university, where he served for twenty-five years as Penn's first professor of physical education. McKenzie was a medical doctor who believed firmly in exercise as a prophylactic measure against health problems. Successfully merging art and anatomy, he produced a series of athletic sculptures early in his career, before expanding into commemorative and memorial commissions, the former including several medallions. His works in Philadelphia include *Young Franklin* (1914), also on the University of Pennsylvania's campus, and *The Ideal Boy Scout* (1937), at 22nd and Winter streets.

Location: 34th Street and Smith Walk, across from the Fisher Fine Arts Library, University of Pennsylvania Campus.

For God and Country. *Photo courtesy of Philadelphia V.A. Medical Center.*

John Harrison, Chemist

John Harrison, Chemist, by Lawrence Tenney Stevens and Frank Lynn Jenkins. *Photo courtesy of Anna Jensky.*

Created by Lawrence Tenney Stevens and Frank Lynn Jenkins, this memorial was originally located at 33rd and Spruce streets, by the university's science building, upon its 1935 installation.

Location: Park near Smith Walk, between 33rd and 34th streets, University of Pennsylvania campus.

For God and Country

This memorial was donated by the American Legion. The inscription on the front of the pedestal reads: FOR GOD AND COUNTRY / WE DEDICATE THIS MEMORIAL / TO THE GALLANT MEN AND / WOMEN OF OUR ARMED FORCES / WHO SERVED THIS GREAT / NATION IN TIME OF PERIL / TO KEEP THIS A FREE NATION / ONE NATION UNDER GOD

Location: V.A. Hospital, 38th Street and Woodland Avenue.

Mario the Magnificent

This 2002 sculpture by Philadelphia artist Eric Berg depicts a ten-foot tall, fourteen-foot long serpentine dragon mounted on an oblong pedestal, and was conceived as a tribute to Drexel University alumnus Mario V. Mascioli, class of 1945. The combined weight of the bronze dragon and the granite pedestal is nearly twenty tons.

Mascioli, who died in January of 2005, served on Drexel's Board of Trustees for nearly twenty-five years, and maintained a lifelong association with his alma mater. For his civic and professional contributions he was inducted in 1994 into the Drexel 100, an organization for distinguished alumni. Mascioli, who held a B.S. in mechanical engineering, was the president of Edmar Abrasive Company, which he founded in 1953. In honor of Mascioli's distinguished service to his community and the University, Drexel changed the name of the school's mascot in 1997 from *The Drexel Dragon* to *Mario the Magnificent*.

Location: 33rd and Market streets, Drexel University campus.

Mario the Magnificent, 2002 by Eric Berg. *Photo courtesy of Stan Horwitz.*

Pan with Sundial
(William Stansfield Memorial)

Created in 1938 by Beatrice Fenton, this memorial sundial was a tribute from the subject's wife.

Location: University of Pennsylvania campus, Locust Walk and 34th Street.

Pan with Sundial. Photo courtesy of Anna Jensky.

Tribute to Nursing

This bronze statue by Philadelphia artist Cathy Hopkins was commissioned by the Presbyterian Medical Center and the Nursing Alumni Association, and unveiled in May of 1989 during National Nurses Week. Hopkins has taught sculpture at the Fleischer Art Memorial, and is currently the chief instructor at Center City Karate.

Location: Presbyterian Medical Center, 38th and Market streets.

Tribute to Nursing, 1989 by Cathy Hopkins. *Photo courtesy of Stan Horwitz.*

William Pepper

William Pepper, M.D., L.L.D, was provost of the University of Pennsylvania for thirteen years. His contemporaries praised him for the school's growth under his leadership, in particular the addition of thirteen departments. Initially, a thirty-two-member "testimonial" committee comprised of his colleagues was formed in April of 1894 to honor the retiring Dr. Pepper. When Pepper died in July of 1898, the proposed testimonial became instead a memorial.

New York sculptor Karl Bitter received a $9,240 commission for the seated bronze of the late provost, which was cast in 1896 by Gorham Manufacturing of Rhode Island. The granite pedestal, designed by Leigh Hunt, has bronze panels on the sides feature bas-reliefs accompanied by quotations from Ralph Waldo Emerson and Benjamin Franklin, respectively. The rear panel lists the new university departments that were a part of Pepper's legacy, along with the apt inscription "You and I must pass away, but these things will last." The memorial was dedicated on December 20th, 1899. A copy was placed inside the main branch of the Free Library of Philadelphia. Pepper was instrumental in founding the library, which was chartered in 1894.

Sculptor Karl Bitter was born in Vienna, Austria, in 1867, and emigrated to New York City in 1889. His list of architectural commissions was as impressive as that of his sculptural ones, the former including a pediment over the main entrance to Philadelphia's 30th Street Station (then known as the Pennsylvania Railroad Station), and decorative panels for the building's interior. Three years prior to that came his big break when he won the competition for one of the three bronze gates for Trinity Church, the theme being man's expulsion from paradise (Gale). Bitter's career was cut short in April of 1915 when he was fatally struck by an automobile when he and his wife, Marie, were leaving the opera. He was forty-seven.

Location: University of Pennsylvania campus, 34th and Spruce streets.

William Pepper. Photo courtesy of Anna Jensky.

Young Franklin

As one of the inscriptions indicates, this memorial is dedicated to the tenth reunion of the class of 1904 of the University of Pennsylvania. Another inscription is a quote from Benjamin Franklin to his son, a quote which epitomizes what the memorial committee intended to express: "I have been the more particular in this description of my journey that you may compare such unlikely beginnings with the figure I have since made there." The young Franklin carries a satchel with his possessions in his right hand, and a simple walking stick in his left. The marble base was designed by architect Paul P. Cret, who, like the sculptor, R. Tait McKenzie, was also a professor at Penn. The June 1914 dedication followed a year after the official groundbreaking.

The idea for a monument to Penn's founder was actually conceived in 1902. The aim was to depict Franklin when he first arrived in Philadelphia in 1723—unknown and penniless—and by so doing inspire future graduates to greatness. Challenges that the planners faced included not only raising the necessary $10,000 for the statue, but determining what a seventeen-year-old Benjamin Franklin would look like.

Founding one of the eight Ivy League schools was only one of Franklin's many legacies. His great success as a publisher and businessman was evidenced in his *Pennsylvania Gazette*—which he purchased in 1729—and his popular magazine, *Poor Richard's Almanack* (1733–1738), in which he offered advice on good health, clean living, and frugality. Many of the maxims first appearing in *Poor Richard's Almanack* are still quoted today. Institutions founded or co-founded by Franklin include the Library Company of Philadelphia (1731), the Philadelphia Union Fire Company (1736), the American Philosophical Society (1743), and the Pennsylvania Hospital (1751) (Independence Hall Association). His accomplishments as an inventor and scientist were equally impressive.

Like many famous individuals, Franklin has occasionally been subjected to posthumous attacks on his character. Among the most common is that he was a shameless womanizer who sired many illegitimate children. While he did father two children out of wedlock, he was hardly the consummate philanderer that some have characterized him. One of those illegitimate children was his son, William, who went on to serve as the royal governor of New Jersey. Once adored by his father, William parted ways with him due to William's loyalist ties during the American Revolution.

Young Franklin. "I have been the more particular in this description of my journey that you may compare such unlikely beginnings with the figure I have since made there." *Photo courtesy of Stan Horwitz.*

Location: In front of Weightman Hall, University of Pennsylvania campus, 33rd and Spruce streets.

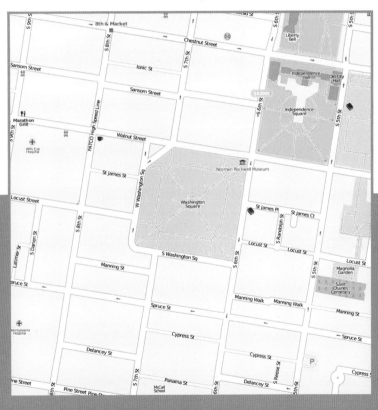

Prisoners of War Memorial

This roughly rectangular rock is affixed with an escutcheon bearing an inscription commemorating American soldiers who died during the Revolutionary War. Though the date on it is October 1900, the plaque appears to be much newer than that.

■ **Location:** Washington Square East, 7th and Walnut streets.

The *Prisoners of War Memorial*, erected October 1900, by the Quaker City Chapter of the Daughters of the American Revolution.

Tomb of the Unknown Soldier

The statue of Washington standing with a cane is a reproduction of a much older example by Jean Antoine Houdon. The encaged eternal flame at the front of the memorial was installed in 1976.

■ **Location:** Washington Square West, 7th and Walnut streets.

Philadelphia's *Tomb of the Unknown Soldier* features a statue of George Washington and a caged eternal flame. *Photo courtesy of Tatiana Heller.*

Anthony J. Drexel

The founder of Drexel University, Anthony J. Drexel also served as the first president of the Fairmount Park Art Association from 1872 until his death in 1893. He was a wealthy banker and philanthropist, for which Drexel University was but one of his legacies. In 1891, he was declared the richest man in Philadelphia, with a net worth of between $25 and $35 million, by the *Philadelphia Inquirer*, which published a list of 160 Philadelphians with assets over one million dollars. By comparison, retail giant John Wanamaker was nineteenth, with approximately three million dollars. Drexel succumbed to a stroke on June 30, 1893, while on his annual vacation in Carlsbad, Germany. He was sixty-six. Tragically, his daughter, Frances Paul, had died the previous year while visiting the German city with him. He was predeceased by his wife, Ellen, but survived by four other children.

This 1904 memorial was created by Sir Moses Jacob Ezekiel from his studio in Rome, and funded by the Paris-based firm of Drexel, Harjes, and Company, in which the late subject had been a partner.

Location: Drexel University Campus, 32nd and Market streets.

The founder of Drexel University, Anthony J. Drexel also served as the first president of the Fairmount Park Art Association from 1872 until his death in 1893. *Photo courtesy of Stan Horwitz.*

Pennsylvania Railroad
War Memorial

Every day, hundreds of travelers, tourists, and transients pass through Amtrak's bustling 30th Street Station, one of three hubs connecting rail passengers to points throughout the city and far beyond. Amazingly, the enormous celestial sculpture at the station's east end sometimes blends unobtrusively into its surroundings, ignored or even missed by busy passers-by. But a few stop to wonder at the thirty-nine-foot bronze statue, and perhaps even to peruse the list of 1,307 names chiseled into the black granite base. Also known as the *Angel of Resurrection*, this monument pays tribute to Pennsylvania Railroad Workers who died during the Second World War, and depicts the Archangel Michael lifting a fallen soldier out of the flames of war. An inscription prefacing the names of the fallen reads: IN MEMORY OF THE MEN AND WOMEN OF THE PENNSYLVANIA RAILROAD WHO LAID DOWN THEIR LIVES FOR OUR COUNTRY 1941–1945. Inscribed on the opposite side of the base is: THAT ALL TRAVELERS HERE MAY REMEMBER THOSE OF THE PENNSYLVANIA RAILROAD WHO DID NOT RETURN FROM THE SECOND WORLD WAR.

The Pennsylvania Railroad War Memorial was unveiled on August 10, 1952, and officially dedicated by World War II General Omar N. Bradley. Bradley, who at the time was chairman of the newly-created Joint Chiefs of Staff, commanded the U.S. II Corps during the Sicily campaign and the 12th U.S. Army Group during the Allied invasion of Nazi-occupied France (USAHEC).

Sculptor Walker Hancock, a Saint Louis native, was a 1924 graduate of the Pennsylvania Academy of Fine Arts, and chaired the school's sculpture department for thirty-six years. Throughout a career that spanned more than eight decades, Hancock created sculptures small and large, from busts of artists and politicians to heroic bronzes of military figures—he even designed medals. His work garnered him numerous awards, among them the Prix de Rome in 1925, the Academy's Gold Medal of Honor in 1953, and the National Medal of Art in 1989. Hancock died in 1999 at the age of ninety-seven.

Location: Inside 30th Street Station, east end of the main concourse, 30th and Market streets.

This monument pays tribute to Pennsylvania Railroad workers who died during the Second World War, and depicts the Archangel Michael lifting a fallen soldier out of the flames of war. *Photo courtesy of Tatiana Heller.*

Stephen Girard

The most recent statue in Philadelphia of Stephen Girard, this one was installed in 1990. The sculptor was Alfred Seebode.

Location: Stephen Girard Park, 21st and Shunk streets.

Stephen Girard, by Alfred Seebode, 1900.

Wynnefield 21

Bishop Matthew Simpson

Photo courtesy of Rev. Dana R. Adam.

Standing tall upon its granite pedestal of commensurate height, this nine-foot bronze statue of Bishop Matthew Simpson was cast in 1897 from a mold designed by sculptor Clark Mills over thirty years prior. The Methodist bishop was originally intended to take his place as one of several sculptures surrounding a central figure of President Abraham Lincoln, as part of a larger monument commemorating the Civil War. Lincoln's untimely death scuttled the project, but the bishop's likeness emerged as its own memorial. The dedication was held on April 2, 1902, on the grounds of the Methodist Episcopal Home for the Aged (now called the Simpson House). Simpson's daughter unveiled the memorial to her father.

A staunch opponent of slavery, Simpson was both a good friend and close advisor to Lincoln, and pulled considerable weight with other members of the president's cabinet, including Secretary of the Treasury (and later Supreme Court Chief Justice) Salmon P. Chase and Secretary of War Edwin M. Stanton. Simpson's influence on the sixteenth president was evidenced by Lincoln's remark, "The Methodist Church, under the leadership of Bishop Simpson, has sent more soldiers to the field, more nurses to the hospital, and more prayers to heaven for the success of our cause than any other church" (Simpson Senior Services). Born in Cadiz, Ohio, on June 21, 1811, Simpson practiced medicine a little, and taught at several universities in addition to his clergy duties. In May of 1852, he was elected bishop. He authored a number of books, some of which comprised collections of his sermons. Simpson delivered the opening oration at the services for the slain President Lincoln on April 19, 1865, in Washington, D.C. Simpson died in Philadelphia on June 18, 1884, and was interred in West Laurel Hill Cemetery.

Location: The Simpson House, Belmont Avenue and Edgely Road.

Bibliography

"3 Philadelphians Killed In Mexico." *Philadelphia Inquirer,* 26 April 1914, 12. NewsBank. 2004. 24 Mar. 2010. infoweb.newsbank.com.

"4 Years & Many Manhours Later." *Chestnut Hill Local,* 7 June 1973.

Abrams, M.H., ed. *The Norton Anthology of English Literature*. 1962. 5th ed., vol. 1. New York: W.W. Norton & Co., 1986, 691, 865-868.

Aero Club of Pennsylvania. Ed. Robert Dant. 6 November 2010 www.aeroclubpa.org.

"Ahron Ben-Shmuel." *James A. Michener Art Museum,* 24 July 2011 www.michenermuseum.org/bucksartists/artist.php?artist=25&page=66.

"Alexander von Humboldt." *Philadelphia Inquirer,* 14 September 1869, 4. Newsbank. 24 January 2011 infoweb.newsbank.com.

"All In Readiness For Unveiling of M'Kinley Statue." *Philadelphia Inquirer,* 6 June 1908, 1. Newsbank, 6 June 2011 infoweb.newsbank.com.

"America's Last Five Star General." U.S. Army Heritage & Education Center (USAHEC), 7 January 2009, 30 November 2010 www.carlisle.army.mil/ahec/AHM/BradleyExhibit/bradleyhome.cfm.

Amorosi, A.D. "A Man of Statue." *City Paper,* 9-15 March 2006. 6 June 2011 archives.citypaper.net/articles/2006-03-09/artpicks5.shtml.

"An Extension Asked." *Philadelphia Inquirer,* 8 November 1891, 2. NewsBank. 2004. 5 July 2011 infoweb.newsbank.com.

An Impartial History of the War in America Between Great Britain and the United States. 2nd ed. Boston, 1783. 367-445. *America's Historical Imprints*. 2005. American Antiquarian Society and NewsBank. 26 March 2011 infoweb.newsbank.com.

"Art Academy Awards European Scholarships." *Philadelphia Inquirer,* 26 May 1916, 4. NewsBank. infoweb.newsbank.com.

"Art Notes." *Philadelphia Inquirer,* 6 May 1894, 13. Newsbank. 2004. 21 March 2010 infoweb.newsbank.com.

"Art Schools Soon Begin Year's Work." *Philadelphia Inquirer,* 25 September 1904, 16. NewsBank. 2004. 26 July 2011 infoweb.newsbank.com.

"A Statue to Goethe." *Philadelphia Inquirer,* 15 November 1887, 2. NewsBank. 2004. 29 June 2011 infoweb.newsbank.com.

A. Thomas Schomberg – Rocky Statue. 8 November 2010 www.rockysculpture.com.

Bach, Penny Balkin. *Public Art in Philadelphia*. Philadelphia: Temple University Press, 1992.

"Background: Franklin Delano Roosevelt Memorial." National Park Service (NPS), 26 August 1997. 25 May 2010 www.nps.gov/ncro/publicaffairs/FDRMemorial.htm.

"Banker Drexel Dies in Europe." *Philadelphia Inquirer,* 1 July 1893, 1. NewsBank. 26 July 2011 infoweb. newsbank.com.

Barnett, Vincent. "Humboldt, Alexander and Wilhelm von." *Europe 1789-1914: Encyclopedia of the Age of Industry and Empire*. Eds. Merriman, John, and Jay Winter. Gale Biography in Context, 24 January 2011 ic.galegroup.com/ic/bic1.

Baym, Nina et al, eds. *The Norton Anthology of American Literature*. 1979. 2nd ed., vol. 1. New York: W.W. Norton & Co., 1985, 359-361, 1960-1968.

Bello, Marisol. "School Hailing Its Larger-Than-Life Hero." *Philadelphia Daily News,* 15 September 1997, 13. Newsbank. 25 December 2010. infoweb. newsbank.com.

"Benjamin Franklin – Craftsman." The Grand Lodge of Free and Accepted Masons of Pennsylvania, 11 November 2010 www.pagrandlodge.org/freemason/0203/bf.html.

Beyond Baseball: The Life of Roberto Clemente. Ed. Parker Hayes. Smithsonian Institution, 26 December 2010 www.robertoclemente.si.edu.

"Biographical Sketch of Raoul Josset." *Texas Archival Resources Online*. The University of Texas at Austin, 19 March 2011 www.lib.utexas.edu/taro/utaaa/00026/aaa-00026.html#bioghist.

Borowski, Neill. "One Liberty Place, With 'Double The Ego Capacity'." *Philadelphia Inquirer,* 12 July 1987, H01. Newsbank. 21 August 2010 infoweb. newsbank.com.

Boston Massacre Historical Society. 2008. 8 March 2011 www.bostonmassacre.net.

Boyer, Deborah. "Statues around Philadelphia, Part One." PhillyHistory.org. City of Philadelphia. 4 July 2009 phillyhistory.org/blog/archive/2009/03/20/statues-around-philadelphia-part-one.aspx.

Brenner, Roslyn F. *Philadelphia's Outdoor Art: A Walking Tour*. 1987. Philadelphia: Camino Books, 2002. 15, 21, 31, 43, 97.

"Bronze Tablet Will Honor Memory Of German Pioneers In America." *Philadelphia Inquirer,* 23 September 1908, 2. NewsBank. 2004. 25 March 2010. infoweb. newsbank.com.

"Bruno, Giordano." *Webster's NewWorld Encyclopedia*. 1992.

Bruno Lucchesi Sculptor. 22 March 2011 www.brunolucchesi.com.

"Buckley Park." *Chestnut Hill Local,* 26 March 1992.

Campbell, W. John. *The Book of Great Books. A Guide to 100 World Classics*. New York: Barnes & Noble Books, 2000, 216-222.

Campisi, Gloria. "Homage to the Memory of Six Million." *Philadelphia Daily News,* 30 April 1984, 16. Newsbank. 8 July 2010 infoweb.newsbank.com.

Campisi, Gloria. "Remembering Ireland's 'Great Hunger'—Famine monument to highlight suffering of the Irish." *Philadelphia Daily News,* 7 February 2002, 14. Newsbank. 26 August 2010 infoweb. newsbank.com.

Caparella, Kitty. "The Art of Readiness At 90, Sculptor's Still Prepared." *Philadelphia Daily News,* 21 November 1991, 50. Newsbank. 28 November 2010 infoweb.newsbank.com.

Caparella, Kitty. "Who's Got 25G Purse For Rocky?" *Philadelphia Daily News*, 30 July 1982, 3. Newsbank. 7 November 2010 infoweb.newsbank.com.

Carter, Joseph C. "Russell H. Conwell." Temple University. 5 July 2011 www.temple.edu/about/RussellConwell.htm.

"Caught on the Fly." *Philadelphia Inquirer*, 4 November 1898, 8. Newsbank. 2004. 15 March 2010 infoweb.newsbank.com.

Chambers II, John Whiteclay. "Pennypacker, Galusha." *The Oxford Companion to Military History*. 1999. *Oxford Reference Online*. Oxford University Press, 17 March 2011 www.oxfordreference.com.

"Charles Dickens." *Webster's New World Encyclopedia*. 1992.

"Chase, Salmon Portland." *Webster's New World Encyclopedia*. 1992.

"Christopher Columbus." *Webster's New World Encyclopedia*. 1992.

"Christopher Columbus Monument." *Philadelphia Inquirer*, 25 September 1876, 2. NewsBank. 2004. 21 March 2010 infoweb.newsbank.com.

"Christopher Columbus Monument." Venturi, Scott Brown and Associates, Inc., 7 December 2010 www.vsba.com/pdfs/ChristopherColumbusMonument01.pdf.

"City Beautiful Pictured in Plans." *Philadelphia Inquirer*, 31 January 1918, 6. Newsbank. 2004. 6 July 2010 infoweb.newsbank.com.

Clements, Adam. "Satterlee General Hospital." Research paper. La Salle University, 22 April 2010. 28 January 2011 uchs.net/pdf/Satterlee_General_Hopital-Adam_Clements.pdf.

"Colossal Figure Cast For Smith Memorial." *Philadelphia Inquirer*, 14 December 1902, 2. Newsbank. 2004. 17 March 2010 infoweb.newsbank.com.

"Columbus Day." Library of Congress American Memory, 6 October 2010. Library of Congress. 6 November 2010 memory.loc.gov/ammem/today/oct12.html.

Committee; Dr. George Logan; Bush Hill; Gerard; Holme.] *National Gazette*, 5 October 1793, 391. NewsBank, 21 March 2011 infoweb.newsbank.com.

"CPI Inflation Calculator." *Bureau of Labor Statistics*. United States Department of Labor, 25 March 2011 data.bls.gov/cgi-bin/cpicalc.pl.

"Czolgosz Has Paid the Penalty of His Awful Crime." *Wilkes-Barre Times*, 29 October 1901, 1. Newsbank, 2004. 27 November 2010 infoweb.newsbank.com.

Dégert, Antoine. "St. Vincent de Paul." *The Catholic Encyclopedia*. Vol. 15. New York: Robert Appleton Company, 1912. 20 July 2011 www.newadvent.org/cathen/15434c.htm.

DeLeon, Clark. "The Scene: Philadelphia and its Suburbs." *Philadelphia Inquirer*, 17 May 1989, B02. 19 July 2011 infoweb.newsbank.com.

Delphi Archaeological Museum. Hellenic Ministry of Culture and Tourism, 2007. 5 March 2011 odysseus.culture.gr.

DeWolf, Rose. "Fairmount Art: The Real Story." *Philadelphia Daily News*, 18 April 1986, 51. Newsbank. 6 July 2010 infoweb.newsbank.com.

Downey, Sally A. "Mario V. Mascioli, 83, firm founder, Drexel booster." *Philadelphia Inquirer*, 20 January 2005, B09. NewsBank. 13 July 2011 infoweb.newsbank.com.

Driscoll, Laura. *Negro Leagues All-Black Baseball*. New York: Grosset and Dunlap, 2002.

Dubin, Murray. "A Hero Of Israel Is Honored With A Phila. Memorial." *Philadelphia Inquirer*, 17 October 1986, B15. Newsbank. 25 April 2011 http:infoweb.newsbank.com.

"Dudley Vaill Talcott." *Contemporary Authors Online*. Detroit: Gale, 1998. Gale Biography in Context, 10 December 2010 ic.galegroup.com/ic/bic1.

Embassy of the Bolivarian Republic of Venezuela. 21 June 2011 venezuela-us.org.

"Everybody's Column." *Philadelphia Inquirer*, 5 May 1922, 12. NewsBank, 2004. 24 March 2010 infoweb.newsbank.com.

Fairmount Park Art Association (FPAA). 2005-2010. 16 October 2010 www.fpaa.org/index.html.

Fairmount Park Art Association (FPAA). *Museum Without Walls*. 2010. 10 November 2010 vimeo.com/12399814.

Fairmount Park Art Association (FPAA). *Sculpture of a City: America's Treasures in Bronze and Stone*. Ed. Nicholas B. Wainwright. Fairmount Park Art Association, 1974.

"Fiancée Mourns Death Of Seaman." *Philadelphia Inquirer*, 26 February 1914, 12. NewsBank, 2004. 22 March 2010 infoweb.newsbank.com.

Fontes, Justine and Ron Fontes. *Abraham Lincoln: Lawyer, Leader, Legend*. London: Dorling Kindersley, Ltd., 2001.

Fox, Steven, Elaine Israel, and Robin O'Callaghan. *The Official SAT Study Guide*. New York: College Board, 2005, 714.

"Franz Schubert." *Classical Net*, 16 July 2011 www.classical.net/music/comp.lst/schubert.php.

"Frederick Graff." *Dictionary of American Biography*. Gale Biography in Context, 23 June 2011 ic.galegroup.com/ic/bic1.

"Friedrich Heinrich Alexander von Humboldt, Baron." *Encyclopedia of World Biography*. Gale Biography in Context, 24 January 2011 ic.galegroup.com/ic/bic1.

"Friends of Charlie Buckley Planning Park in His Honor." *Chestnut Hill Local*, 20 April 1969.

"Funeral of General Reilly." *Philadelphia Inquirer*, 4 March 1896, 4. NewsBank. 2004. 22 March 2010 infoweb.newsbank.com.

"Galileo Galilei." *Webster's New World Encyclopedia*, 1992.

"Germantown Pays Founders Homage." *Philadelphia Inquirer*, 11 November 1920, 4. NewsBank, 2004. 25 March 2010 infoweb.newsbank.com.

"Germantown Split on Park Monument." *Philadelphia Inquirer*, 5 April 1906, 6. Newsbank. 4 November 2010 infoweb.newsbank.com.

"Girard's Memory is Duly Honored. Bronze Statue Unveiled in the Presence of Thousands of People." *Philadelphia Inquirer*, 21 May 1897, 1. NewsBank. 1 April 2011 infoweb.newsbank.com.

"Goethe." *The New Encyclopaedia Brittanica* 20, 2007.

"Goethe's Monument." *Philadelphia Inquirer*, 31 May 1891, 7. NewsBank, 2004. 29 June 2011 <infoweb. newsbank.com.

Goldwyn, Ron. "Korea Vets Remember the 'Forgotten War'." *Philadelphia Daily News*, 28 May 2002, 7. NewsBank infoweb.newsbank.com.

Goodman, Howard. "A Super Salute To Discovery. America's Birthplace Is Throwing The Biggest Columbus Parade Of The Year To Celebrate A Voyage That Set The World On Its Ear." *Philadelphia Inquirer*, 9 October 1992, 18. Newsbank. 16 December 2010 infoweb.newsbank.com.

"Grace Kelly." *Webster's New World Encyclopedia*. 1992.

Gralish, Tom. "Restoring a grand gateway." *Philadelphia Inquirer*, 10 January 2004, B01. Newsbank. 7 July 2010 infoweb.newsbank.com.

"Grand New Memorial Arch in the Park." *Philadelphia Inquirer*, 27 November 1898, 9. Newsbank, 2004. 16 March 2010 infoweb.newsbank.com.

Greenthal, Kathryn. "French, Daniel Chester." *Oxford Art Online*, 27 September 1999. Oxford University Press, 27 December 2010 www.oxfordartonline. com.

"Greet Oar Champions. Falls of Schuylkill Welcomes Kelly and Costello." *Philadelphia Inquirer*, 23 September 1920, 2. Newsbank. 15 November 2010 infoweb. newsbank.com.

"Grim Reaper's Weekly Harvest." *Philadelphia Inquirer*, 10 June 1910, 8. NewsBank, 2004. 29 March 2010 infoweb.newsbank.com.

"Guglielmo Marconi – Biography." *Nobelprize.org*. 18 July 2011 nobelprize.org/nobel_prizes/physics/ laureates/1909/marconi.html.

"Guglielmo Marconi – Nobel Lecture." *Nobelprize.org*. 18 July 2011 nobelprize.org/nobel_prizes/physics/ laureates/1909/marconi.html.

Hanson, Cynthia. "Kin Seek Memorial To Marines." *Philadelphia Inquirer*, 2 June 1986, B16. NewsBank. 11 July 2011 infoweb.newsbank.com.

Harley, Lewis R. "Old Trappe Church One of the Most Interesting Edifices in the Keystone State." *Philadelphia Inquirer*, 26 April 1891, 9. NewsBank. 29 March 2011 infoweb.newsbank.com.

"Henry Mitchell. Philadelphia Sculptor. 1915-1980." Ed. John Guinee. 29 May 2011 henrywmitchell.com.

"Heroic Bronze of Martyred President Erected on City Hall Plaza Awaiting Unveiling." *Philadelphia Inquirer*, 13 May 1908, 2. Newsbank. 27 November 2010 infoweb.newsbank.com.

Hine, Thomas. "1 Percent Solution: Endowing The City With A Wealth Of Art." *Philadelphia Inquirer*, 5 December 1983, D01. 27 March 2011 nl.newsbank. com/nl-search/we/Archives.

Hine, Thomas. "A Phila. Salute to Columbus." *Philadelphia Inquirer*, 22 December 1991, F01. Newsbank. 16 December 2010 infoweb.newsbank.com.

History of the Free Library of Philadelphia." Free Library of Philadelphia, 1 February 2011 www.freelibrary. org/about/history.htm.

Homan, Lynn M. and Thomas Reilly. *Visiting Turn-of-the-Century Philadelphia*. Charleston, SC: Arcadia Publishing, 1999, 56-57.

Hopko, Thomas. *Bible and Church History*. 1973. 6th ed., vol. iii. New York: Orthodox Church in America, 2005, 163.

Iams, David. "Gimbel Award Phila. Tradition To Continue, Sponsored By Hospital." *Philadelphia Inquirer*, 6 February 1987. *Philly.com article collections*. 1 April 2011 articles.philly.com/1987-02-06/ news/26176663_1_award-winners-past-recipients-international-awards.

"Ida Saxton McKinley." *The White House*, 26 November 2010 www.whitehouse.gov/about/first-ladies/ idamckinley.

[Incorporated German Society. . .] *Poulson's American Daily Advertiser*, 6 October 1807, 3. NewsBank, 2004. 29 March 2010 infoweb.newsbank.com.

"In The Nation And The World." *Philadelphia Inquirer*, 4 January 1999, B05. Newsbank. 29 November 2010 infoweb.newsbank.com.

"James Garfield." *The White House*, 31 July 2010 www. whitehouse.gov/about/presidents/jamesgarfield.

"John Brendan Kelly." *Dictionary of American Biography*. New York: Charles Scribner's Sons, 1980. Gale Biography In Context, 22 November 2010 ic.galegroup.com/ic/bic1.

"John Marshall." *ushistory.org*, 1995. Independence Hall Association. 15 January 2011 www.ushistory.org/ valleyforge/served/marshall.html.

"John Wanamaker." *PBS*, 12 June 2011 www.pbs.org/wgbh/ theymadeamerica/whomade/wanamaker_hi.html.

"John Wister." *The National Encyclopaedia of American Biography*. Vol. XXXIV. New York: James T. White & Co., 1948. 25 January 2010 www.ushistory.org/ germantown/people/wister.htm.

"John Witherspoon." *Encyclopedia of World Biography*. Detroit: Gale, 1988. Gale U.S. History in Context, 1 July 2011 ic.galegroup.com/ic/uhic.

"Jonsson, Einar." *Oxford Art Online*, 2007-2010. 18 December 2010 www.oxfordartonline.com.

"Joseph Leidy (1823-1891): Encyclopedist of the Natural World." The Academy of Natural Sciences, 21 May 2011 www.ansp.org/museum/leidy/index.php.

"Jottings About The City." *Philadelphia Inquirer* 7 May, 1889, 3. NewsBank. 2004. 29 Jun. 2011 infoweb. newsbank.com.

"Jottings About The City." *Philadelphia Inquirer*, 25 December 1890, 1. NewsBank, 2004. 29 June 2011 infoweb.newsbank.com.

Journal of the Common Council of the City of Philadelphia From June 1, 1911 to November 28, 1911. Vol. III. Philadelphia: Dunlap Printing Co., 1911, 35-36.

"Karl Theodore Francis Bitter." *Dictionary of American Biography*. New York: Charles Scribner's Sons, 1936. Gale Biography in Context, 1 February 2011 ic.galegroup.com/ic/bic1.

Kaufman, Marc. "Dilworth Memorial Unveiled, Though A Bit Too Late For Some." *Philadelphia Inquirer*, 5 November 1982, B08. Newsbank. 19 April 2011 infoweb.newsbank.com.

Kelly, John Barry. "Commodore Barry." *ushistory.org*, 1995. Independence Hall Association. 27 June 2010 www.ushistory.org/people/commodorebarry.htm.

Ketchum, Richard M., ed. *The American Heritage Book of the Revolution*. New York: American Heritage Publishing Co., Inc., 1958, 20-21, 46, 110, 128, 213-216, 219, 266, 322.

Khoren Der Harootian Armenian American Artist. Amped Media. 7 March 2011 www.derharootian.com.

Kindig, Thomas E. "Robert Morris." *ushistory.org*, 1995. Independence Hall Association. 22 May 2010 www.ushistory.org/declaration/signers/morris_r.htm.

"Kosciuszko Tadeusz." *Webster's New World Encyclopedia*, 1992.

Krotzer, Dorothy. "War Memorial." *Friends of Gorgas Park*, 2010. The Friends of Gorgas Park. 5 February 2011 www.gorgaspark.com/memorial/memorial.html.

"Lawmakers Busy at Harrisburg." *Philadelphia Inquirer*, 22 February 1903, 9. Newsbank. 3 November 2010 infoweb.newsbank.com.

"LEFT MUCH TO CHARITY." *Philadelphia Inquirer*, 30 January 1906, 15. NewsBank, 2004. 5 July 2011 infoweb.newsbank.com.

"Leonard Baskin (1922-2000)." *Galerie St. Etienne*, 25 May 2011 www.gseart.com.

"Lewis Iselin, 77, Dies; Sculptor of Portraits." *New York Times*, 11 August 1990. 14 March 2011 www.nytimes.com/1990/08/11/obituaries/lewis-iselin-77-dies-sculptor-of-portraits.html.

"Lewis Iselin Interview, 1969 April 10." *Archives of American Art*, 2011. Smithsonian Institution. 14 March 2011 www.aaa.si.edu/collections/interviews/lewis-iselin-interview-11962.

Lindsay Daen Bronze Sculptor. Ed. Carolyn B. Beale. 29 March 2011 lindsaydaen.com.

Lloyd, June. "Artist Charles Rudy, Native of York, Was Very Talented and Versatile." 22 March 2010. 6 July 2011 www.yorkblog.com/universal/2010/03/artist-charles-rudy-native-of.html.

Mackay, James. *The Dictionary of Sculptors in Bronze*. Woodbridge, England: Antique Collectors' Club, 1977.

"MacNeil, Hermon Atkins." *The Metropolitan Museum of Art*. 17 March 2011 www.metmuseum.org/toah/hi/hi_macneilhermonatkins.htm.

Madueño, Elena. "Fitzsimmons (Fitzsimons), Thomas." *Pennsylvania Center for the Book*. The Pennsylvania State University. 31 May 2011 pabook.libraries.psu.edu/palitmap/bios/Fitzsimmons__Thomas.html.

Magner, Blake A. *At Peace With Honor: The Civil War Burials of Laurel Hill Cemetery Philadelphia, Pennsylvania*. Collingswood, NJ: C. W. Historicals, 28-30.

Marder, Dianna. "Rizzo's 1980 Cadillac sold at auction – Hizzoner's statue needed the dough." *Philadelphia Inquirer*, 26 September 2010, B01. Newsbank. 2 January 2011 infoweb.newsbank.com.

Marquez, Steven A. "Memorial Planned For Beirut Marines." *Philadelphia Daily News*, NewsBank. 3 June 1986 infoweb.newsbank.com.

"Mayor Gives Hillers Buckley Park Citation." *Chestnut Hill Local*, 22 July, 1976.

"Mayors of the City of Philadelphia 1691-2000." *City of Philadelphia*, 13 January 1998. 3 June 2010. www.phila.gov/PHILS/Mayorlst.htm.

"The M'clellan Statue." *Philadelphia Inquirer*, 18 September 1894, Newsbank, 2004. 21 March 2010 infoweb.newsbank.com.

"McKinley Monument Finished." *Philadelphia Inquirer*, 19 April 1908, 1. Newsbank. 27 November 2010 infoweb.newsbank.com.

McSpadden, J. Walker. *Famous Sculptors of America*. 1924. Freeport, NY: Books for Libraries Press, 1968, 247-273.

Meltzer, Marc. "Feast For The Eyes. Penn's Landing To Be Site Of Memorial To Potato Famine." *Philadelphia Daily News*, 23 November 1999, 27. Newsbank. 26 August 2010 infoweb.newsbank.com.

"Metropolitan Andrey Sheptytsky." *Metropolitan Andrey Sheptytsky Institute of Eastern Christian Studies*, 2010. 27 June 2011 www.sheptytskyinstitute.ca/?page_id=6.

Milano, Kenneth W. *The History of Penn Treaty Park*. Charleston, SC: The History Press, 2009, 9, 10, 15, 21, 23, 25, 55, 85, 133-137, 141, 143, 146, 150-153.

"Monster Parade Precedes Unveiling at City Hall." *Philadelphia Inquirer*, 7 October 1910, 1-2. NewsBank, 2004. 29 March 2010 infoweb.newsbank.com.

"Monuments, Memorials and Cemeteries of the AEF." *World War I Trenches on the Web*. Ed. Mike Hanlon. 3 June 2004. 3 July 2009 www.worldwar1.com/dbc/monument.htm.

Morgan, Ann Lee. "MacNeil, Hermon Atkins." *The Oxford Dictionary of American Art and Artists*, 2007. *Oxford Reference Online*. Oxford University Press, 17 March 2011 www.oxfordreference.com.

National Governors Association. 2010. 9 June 2010 www.nga.org.

National Sculpture Society. 23 December 2010 www.nationalsculpture.org.

Naude, Virginia Norton, ed. *Sculptural Monuments In An Outdoor Environment*. Philadelphia: Pennsylvania Academy of the Fine Arts, 1985. 12, 54, 106, 107.

Nelson, Paul. "Anthony Wayne." *Encyclopedia of the American Revolution: Library of Military History*. Ed. Harold E. Selesky. Detroit: Charles Scribner's Sons, 2006. Gale Biography in Context, 12 March 2011 ic.galegroup.com/ic/bic1.

"New Publications. The Life of Bishop Matthew Simpson by Rev. Dr. Crooks." *Philadelphia Inquirer*, 14 April 1890, 6. NewsBank. infoweb.newsbank.com.

"News of Art and Artists." *Philadelphia Inquirer*, 16 December 1906, 5. NewsBank, 2004. 27 November 2010 infoweb.newsbank.com.

Nicholson, Jim. "Reginald Beauchamp, Creative Building Exec." *Philadelphia Daily News*, 26 December 2000, 52. NewsBank. 16 May 2011 infoweb.newsbank.com.

"Nicolaus Copernicus." *Scientists: Their Lives and Works*, 2006. Gale Biography in Context, 10 December 2010 ic.galegroup.com/ic/bic1.

Obituary for Henry Melchior Muhlenberg. *The Independent Gazetteer*, 26 October 1787, 2. NewsBank, 2004. 24 March 2010. infoweb.newsbank.com.

Obituary for Herman Kirn. *Philadelphia Inquirer*, 23 July 1920, 9. NewsBank. 19 March 2011 infoweb. newsbank.com.

Obituary for Stephen Girard. *National Gazette And Literary Register*, 29 December 1831, 2. NewsBank. 21 March 2011 infoweb.newsbank.com.

Obituary for T. Waldo Story. *Philadelphia Inquirer*, 24 October 1915, 12. NewsBank, 2004. 29 March 2010 infoweb.newsbank.com.

"Oil Paintings Of the Old and Modern Schools Belonging to the Estate of the late Meta J. Conor-Wood." *The Evening Post*, 27 January 1918, 9. 23 July 2011 fultonhistory.com.

Olley, Christine. "Philly cops lost in 2008 honored at annual Living Flame memorial." *Philadelphia Daily News*, 7 May 2009, 7. Newsbank. 16 May 2011 infoweb.newsbank.com.

"Olympic Games." *Webster's New World Encyclopedia*, 1992.

"Opening Address. Remarks of General Wagner, President of the Board of City Trusts." *Philadelphia Inquirer*, 21 May 1897, 11. Newsbank. infoweb.newsbank.com.

Opper, Thorsten. "Delphi Charioteer." 14 May 2009. *Oxford Art Online*. Oxford University Press. 4 March 2010 www.oxfordartonline.com.

"Our Fountains and Their Histories." *Philadelphia Inquirer*, 24 May 1896, 25. Newsbank. 2004. 17 March 2010 infoweb.newsbank.com.

Paolantonio, S.A., Doreen Carvajal, Marc DuVoisin and Richard Burke. "Rendell Wins In A Landslide Egan Falls By 2-1." *Philadelphia Inquirer*, 6 November 1991, A01. Newsbank. 3 January 2011 infoweb. newsbank.com.

"Peking Says It Will Talk About Cultural Ties To U.S." *Philadelphia Inquirer*, 30 December 1983, A10. Newsbank. 16 August 2010 infoweb.newsbank.com.

Penn University Archives & Records Center. University of Pennsylvania University Archives and Records Center. 10 January 2011 www.archives.upenn.edu.

"Philadelphia and Suburbs. Street Fountains." *Philadelphia Inquirer*, 12 June 1873, 3. Newsbank, 2004. 17 March 2010 infoweb.newsbank.com.

Philadelphia Public Art. Ed. Chris Purdom. 31 January 2010. 4 February 2010 www.philart.net.

Philadelphia Vietnam Veterans Memorial. 2008. Philadelphia Vietnam Veterans Memorial Fund. 20 August 2010 pvvm.org.

"Philip Price, Lawyer, Park Commissioner." *Philadelphia Daily News*, 11 May 1989, 59. NewsBank. 30 March 2011 infoweb.newsbank.com.

"Plan Big Tribute For Dead Heroes." *Philadelphia Inquirer*, 27 April 1914, 3. NewsBank, 2004. 24 March 2010 infoweb.newsbank.com.

"Plan Memorial For Hero." *Philadelphia Inquirer*, 25 May 1916, 10. NewsBank, 2004. 24 March 2010 infoweb. newsbank.com.

Plimpton, Ruth. *Mary Dyer: Biography of a Rebel Quaker*. Boston: Brandon Publishing Co., 1994, 11-13.

Polish American Bicentennial Committee of Philadelphia. *A Guide And Directory Of Philadelphia And Its Polonia 1976*. Philadelphia, 1976.

Poles in America Foundation, Inc. Ed. Edward Pinkowski. 20 December 2010 www.poles.org

Pray, Rusty. "One of the great citizens of Phila." *Philadelphia Inquirer*, 12 August 2005, A01. NewsBank. 31 March 2011 nl.newsbank.com/nl-search/we/Archives.

Public Art in Philadelphia. Ed. Max Buten. 7 December 2010 www.pbase.com/mistermax/philart&page=all.

"Pulaski, Casimir." *Webster's New World Encyclopedia*, 1992.

"Pythian Games." *Webster's New World Encyclopedia*, 1992.

"Quaker Mary Dyer." *Mass.gov*, 2010. Commonwealth of Massachusetts. 11 December 2010 www.mass.gov.

"R. Tait McKenzie Statue." *Cradle of Liberty Council, Boy Scouts of America*, 25 June 2011 colbsa.org/openrosters/ViewOrgPageLink. asp?LinkKey=2327&orgkey=541.

Raid on Entebbe. Dir. Irvin Kershner. Perf. Yaphet Kotto, Charles Bronson. NBC, 1976.

"Robert Indiana." *Scribner Encyclopedia of American Lives, Thematic Series: Sports Figures*. Ed. Arnold Markoe and Kenneth T. Jackson. New York: Charles Scribner's Sons, 2003. Gale Biography In Context. 21 November 2010. ic.galegroup.com/ic/bic1.

"Rocky." *Internet Movie Database*. 8 November 2010 www. imdb.com.

Russ, Valeria. "Goode Praises 'Friendship Gate'." *Philadelphia Daily News*, 26 January 1984, 31. Newsbank. 7 July 2010 infoweb.newsbank.com.

Salisbury, Stephan. "Joan of Arc returns to perch outside Art Museum." *Philadelphia Inquirer*, 22 April 2010, B01.

Salisbury, Stephan. "Rizzo The Statue To Some, The 10-Foot Tall Memorial Is Not Arresting Enough. But Maybe It's Not Possible To Capture In A Figurative Statue The Essence Of The Big Bambino." *Philadelphia Inquirer*, 19 January 1999, E01. 1 January 2011 infoweb.newsbank.com.

"Sarah Dickson Lowrie Biography of Eli Kirk Price: Historical Note." *Philadelphia Museum of Art*, 30 March 2011 www.philamuseum.org/pma_archives/ead.php?c=LOW&p=hn.

Schanzer, Rosalyn. *How Ben Franklin Stole the Lightning*. Harper Collins Publishers, 2003.

Schuylkill Navy, Philadelphia. *Constitution, by-laws and rules of the Schuylkill Navy of Philadelphia (1876)*. Library of Congress. *Internet Archive*. 25 July 2011 www. archive.org/stream/constitutionbyla00schu#page/n9/mode/2up.

"Sculpture Shapes Up For A Big Day." *Philadelphia Inquirer*, 21 June 1995, B01. 15 May 2011 infoweb. newsbank.com.

"Seven Years' War." *The Dictionary of Cultural Literacy*, 1993, 2nd ed.

"Shopkeeper Starts Park Fund Drive To Continue May 3 & 4." *Chestnut Hill Local*, 24 April 1969.

Shotgun's Home of the American Civil War, 2 September 2008. 27 October 2010 www.civilwarhome.com.

"Simpson House History." *Simpson Senior Services*. 23 January 2011 www.simpsonsenior.org.

Sims, Gayle Ronan. "S. C. Soong – designed famed gate." *Philadelphia Inquirer*, 20 April 2006, B08. Newsbank. 15 August 2010 infoweb.newsbank.com.

"Single Monument to Mark Battle." *Philadelphia Inquirer*, 3 August 1903, 7. Newsbank. 3 November 2010 infoweb.newsbank.com.

Skaler, Robert Morris and Thomas H. Keels. *Philadelphia's Rittenhouse Square*. Charleston, SC: Arcadia Publishing, 2008, 87.

"Society Honors Father Matthew." *Philadelphia Inquirer*, 31 May 1911, 2. NewsBank. 19 March 2011 infoweb. newsbank.com.

Sokolove, Michael, Marjorie Valbrun, and Emilie Lounsberry. "Columbus Day Parade Sails Along Smoothly The Day Wasn't Without Incident. A New Monument Was Splattered With Paint." *Philadelphia Inquirer*, 12 October 1992, B01. Newsbank. 17 December 2010 infoweb.newsbank.com.

Speers, W. et al. "Hall Sees Wedding March With Jagger." *Philadelphia Daily News*, 19 January 1990, D02. Newsbank. 7 November 2010 infoweb.newsbank. com.

Stanley, Lea Sitton. "Making A Dream Come True In Bronze A Statue Memorializing Roberto Clemente Carries A Message To Children." *Philadelphia Inquirer*, 16 September 1997, B01. Newsbank. 25 December 2010 infoweb.newsbank.com.

"Stanton, Edwin McMasters." *Webster's New World Encyclopedia*, 1992.

"Statues of Heroes To Be Erected Under General Reilly's Will." *Philadelphia Inquirer*, 4 September 1897, 3. Newsbank. 2004. 22 March 2010 infoweb.newsbank.com.

"Stephen Girard." *Girard College*. 2002-2008. 22 March 2011 www.girardcollege.com.

Stoiber, Julie. "Inspired by a likeness, Philadelphians celebrate novelist's birthday." Knight Ridder/Tribune News Service, 2001. HighBeam Research. 25 January 2010 www.highbeam.com/doc/1G1-70715303.html.

Stoiber, June. "Partnerships help preserve public art—Philadelphia simply cannot afford to maintain donated war memorials and other monuments." *Philadelphia Inquirer*, 7 November 2004, B05. Newsbank. 7 November 2010 infoweb.newsbank. com.

"St. Patrick's Sons Honor 'Fighting John' Barry by Unveiling Statue in Independence Square." *Philadelphia Inquirer*, 17 March 1907, 1, 8. Newsbank, 2004. 15 March 2010 infoweb.newsbank.com.

Summit Educational Group. *The SAT & PSAT Course Book*. Newton, MA: Summit Educational Group, 2008, 63.

Supreme Court of the United States. 14 January 2011 www. supremecourt.gov.

"Terrorist Attacks on Americans, 1979-1988." *PBS*. 12 July 2011 www.pbs.org/wgbh/pages/frontline/shows/target/etc/cron.html.

The Armenian Genocide. Writer Andrew Goldberg. DVD. Oregon Public Broadcasting (OPB), 2005.

"The Benjamin Franklin National Memorial." *The Franklin Institute*. 9 March 2011 www2.fi.edu/exhibits/permanent/franklin_national_memorial.php.

"The Centennial Fountain." *Philadelphia Inquirer*, 23 February 1875, 2. NewsBank. 19 March 2011 infoweb.newsbank.com.

The District Reports Of Cases Decided In All The Judicial Districts Of The State of Pennsylvania During the Year 1911. Vol. XX. Philadelphia: Howard W. Page, 1911, 334.

The Double Life of Franz Schubert. Writer Nicholas Kent. DVD. Kultur International Films, 1997.

The Einar Jonsson Museum. 18 December 2010 www. skulptur.is.

"The Electric Benjamin Franklin." *ushistory.org*, 1998-2010. Independence Hall Association. 11 January 2010 www.ushistory.org/franklin/info/index.htm.

"The Forgotten Humboldt." *Philadelphia Inquirer*, 18 May 1904, 8. NewsBank. 23 January 2011 infoweb. newsbank.com.

"The German Poet." *Philadelphia Inquirer*, 11 November 1885, 2. NewsBank, 2004. 29 June 2011 infoweb. newsbank.com.

"The Goliad Massacre." *Presidio La Bahia*, 2002. 19 March 2011 www.presidiolabahia.org/massacre.htm.

The History Channel Presents: The American Revolution. Prod. Scott Paddor. 1994. DVD (five discs). Greystone Communications.

The Holy Scriptures. 1917. Philadelphia: Jewish Publication Society of America, 1955. 367, 989.

The Irish Memorial. 3 July 2009 www.irishmemorial.org.

"The Late Wm. J. Horstmann." *Philadelphia Inquirer*, 27 May 1872, 3. NewsBank. 23 January 2011 infoweb. newsbank.com.

"The Liberty Bell." *ushistory.org*, 1998-2010. Independence Hall Association. 1 July 2010 www.ushistory.org/libertybell/index.html.

"The Martyred Maid Fremiet's Beautiful Statue of Joan of Arc Unveiled." *The Philadelphia Inquirer*, 16 November 1890, 8. NewBank, 2004. 22 March 2010 infoweb.newsbank.com.

"The Millionaires of Our City." *Philadelphia Inquirer*, 14 June 1891, 6. NewsBank, 2004 infoweb.newsbank. com.

"The Monument to William Pepper, M.D., L.L.D. Its Inception, Completion and Presentation 1894-1899." *University of Pennsylvania Libraries*, 2 April 2003. University of Pennsylvania. 1 February 2011 www.library.upenn.edu/exhibits/pennhistory/pepper/pepper.memorial.html.

"The Old Curiosity Shop." *Charles Dickens Online*. 14 August 2010 www.dickenslit.com/Old_Curiosity_Shop/index.html.

The Philadelphia Award. 30 March 2011 www.philaaward. org.

"The President's Body Coming to Philadelphia." *Philadelphia Inquirer*, 20 April 1865, 1. NewsBank. 23 January 2011 infoweb.newsbank.com.

"The Satterlee Hospital." *Philadelphia Inquirer*, 2 June 1863, 1. NewsBank. 29 January 2011 infoweb. newsbank.com.

"Thomas Fitzsimons." *Dictionary of American Biography*. New York: Charles Scribner's Sons, 1936. *Gale U.S. History In Context*. 31 May 2011 ic.galegroup.com/ic/uhic.

"To Unveil Barry Memorial Statue." *Philadelphia Inquirer*, 4 March 1907, 15. Newsbank, 2004. 15 March 2010 infoweb.newsbank.com.

Trujillo, Carla and Charlene Mires. "Patriots of African Descent Monument." *Valley Forge National Historical Park*. National Park Service (NPS). 6 June 2011 www.nps.gov/vafo/historyculture/africanpatriotsmonument.htm.

"Two Philadelphia Mothers Receive Their Dead Sons." *Philadelphia Inquirer*, 12 May 1914, 1. NewsBank, 2004. 24 March 2010 infoweb.newsbank.com.

"University Friends Fittingly Honored." *Philadelphia Inquirer*, 29 April 1901, 9. NewsBank, 2004. 5 July 2011 infoweb.newsbank.com.

"UNVEILING LEIDY STATUE." *Philadelphia Inquirer*, 15 October 1907, 6. NewsBank. 20 May 2011 infoweb.newsbank.com.

"Unveiled Statue To Bishop Simpson." *Philadelphia Inquirer*, 3 April 1902. NewsBank. 23 January 2011 infoweb.newsbank.com.

Van Atta, Burr. "Gerd Utescher, 71, Sculptor of 'Freedom Fountain' in City." *Philadelphia Inquirer*, 1 April 1983, B07. NewsBank. 18 May 2011 infoweb.newsbank.com.

Vance, Donna Williams. "Art Museum Spotlights The Lipchitz Collection." *Philadelphia Daily News*, 30 June 2004, 51. NewsBank. 6 January 2011 infoweb.newsbank.com.

"Vera Cruz Victims Share Honor Given To Nation's Elect." *Philadelphia Inquirer*, 14 May 1914, 1. NewsBank, 2004. 24 March 2010 infoweb.newsbank.com.

Verdi: The Pursuit and Burden of Success. Narrator Mark Elder. DVD. Vasconcellos, 1994.

Monsieur Vincent. Perf. Pierre Fresnay, Jean Carmet. 1947. DVD. Studio Canal.

Von Steuben, Frederick William Baron. *Baron von Steuben's Revolutionary War Drill Manual. A Facsimile Reprint of the 1794 Edition*. 1985.

Wallace, Andy. "Emlen Etting, 87, Artist, Poet, Perennial Fixture of Social Scene." *Philadelphia Inquirer*, 23 July 1993, B06. NewsBank. 19 April 2011 infoweb.newsbank.com.

Warner, Bob. "City Hopes China Won't Slam Gate." *Philadelphia Daily News*, 8 April 1983, 16. Newsbank. 7 July 2010 infoweb.newsbank.com.

"Washington Monument." *Philadelphia Inquirer*, 27 June 1891, 1. Newsbank, 2004. 5 July 2010 infoweb.newsbank.com.

"Waugh, Captain Sidney Blehler." *Monuments Men Foundation for the Preservation of Art*, 2007. 22 December 2010 https://www.monumentsmenfoundation.org/monumentsmen/default.aspx#315.

Wilkinson, Alan G. "Lipchitz, Jacques." *Oxford Art Online*. Oxford University Press. 6 January 2011 www.oxfordartonline.com.

"William McKinley." *The White House*. 26 November 2010 www.whitehouse.gov/about/presidents/williammckinley.

"William McKinley." *Historic World Leaders*. 1994. Gale Biography in Context. 26 November 2010 ic.galegroup.com/ic/bic1.

"William Wetmore Story." *Philadelphia Inquirer*, 24 April 1892, 16. NewsBank, 2004. 29 March 2010 infoweb.newsbank.com.

Wooster, Robert. *Civil War 100*. Seacaucus, N.J.: Carol Publishing Group, 1998, 7-9, 24-26, 175-177.

Yant, Monica. "Quixote Statue Is Bid To Inspire Area To Dream." *Philadelphia Inquirer*, 10 November 1997, B01. Newsbank. 19 January 2011 infoweb.newsbank.com.

Yockelson, Mitchell. "The United States Armed Forces and the Mexican Punitive Expedition: Part 1." *Prologue Magazine* Fall, 1997. *The National Archives*. The National Archives and Records Administration. 11 August 2010 www.archives.gov.

Zenos Frudakis. 4 January 2011 www.zenosfrudakis.com.

Index